PAT BROWN, MBA

Financial Literacy For NIL for International Student Athletes

"The International Student-Athlete's Playbook for Building Wealth, Protecting Status, and Navigating NIL"

ABRAM 47 BROWN

First published by AbramBrown47 2025

First edition

ISBN: 978-1-967737-06-2

This book was professionally typeset on Reedsy.
Find out more at reedsy.com

Contents

Preface v
Quick Note.. vii
How to Use This Book viii
How This Book Connects to the Full NIL Financial Literacy... x
SECTION I: INTRODUCTION 1
Chapter 1: Why This Book Matters 4
Chapter 2: Understanding NIL as an International... 10
Chapter 3: Know Your Visa — F-1, CPT, OPT & NIL 16
Chapter 4: Pros and Cons of NIL for International Athletes 22
SECTION II: Visas & Compliance 27
Chapter 5: Budgeting Basics — The "Practice Plan" for Your... 30
Chapter 6: Understanding Credit in the U.S. 34
Chapter 7: Making NIL Work (Legally & Smartly) 39
SECTION III: Money 101 for International Athletes 45
Chapter 8: Taxes & Reporting Income 50
Chapter 9: NIL Branding for International Athletes 55
Chapter 10: Business Structures & Agents 59
Chapter 11: International NIL Readiness Checklist 63
Chapter 12: Understanding Currency Exchange and... 66
SECTION IV: NIL Income — Getting It, Managing It, Reporting... 73
Chapter 13: Social Media Safety, Sponsorship Etiquette, and... 77
Chapter 14: NIL and Education – Balancing Academics,... 83
Chapter 15: Networking in the NIL Era – Relationships That... 89
Chapter 16: Life After College – What Happens to Your NIL... 95
SECTION V: Building Your Brand & Business Acumen 100
Chapter 17: NIL for Women in International Sports 103

Chapter 18: NIL and Mental Health – Protecting Your Mind... 108
Chapter 19: Managing Peer Pressure and Lifestyle Inflation 115
Chapter 20: How to Vet Professionals—Agents, Advisors, and... 119
Chapter 21: NIL and Taxes in Your Home Country 124
Chapter 22: Creating a Legacy with NIL – Giving Back and... 129
Chapter 23: Banking and Investing — How to Open the Right... 133
Chapter 24: NIL Stories From International Athletes 138
SECTION VI: SPORTS-SPECIFIC STRATEGIES 142
Chapter 25: Planning for Professional Sports (Domestic &... 148
Chapter 26: NIL and the Transfer Portal 153
Chapter 27: Car Chase 158
Chapter 28: Content Across Borders — Creating,... 162
Chapter 29: How Investing Works – Making Your Money Work... 168
Chapter 30: You Love Them. But You Can't Save Them All. 173
Chapter 31: What Is the Market, the Economy, and Everything... 179
Chapter 32: How to Start Investing – Your NIL Playbook for... 188
Chapter 33: Wrong Examples 194
Chapter 34: What's a Portfolio? Build Your Game Plan,... 198
Chapter 35: The Eighth Wonder of the World – Understanding... 204
Chapter 36: The Power of No – Protecting Your Peace and Your... 211
Chapter 30: You Made It Here—Now Make It Count: The Legacy... 219
Disclaimer 225
Questions to ask 226
Important Financial Dates for International Students 229
Money & Banking Terms 232
About the Author 235

Preface

When Name, Image, and Likeness (NIL) opportunities became a reality in the United States, the college sports world changed overnight. For the first time in history, student-athletes could legally earn income from their personal brand while still competing at the amateur level. But for international student-athletes, the road has been far more complicated.

This book was created specifically for you—the international student-athlete living thousands of miles from home, adjusting to a new country, and now being introduced to a financial system that's complex, fast-moving, and sometimes hard to navigate. You didn't just come here to compete; you came here to grow. And now, NIL has added a new dimension to your journey.

As the global sports world continues to evolve, international athletes are increasingly in the spotlight. You're bringing more than talent—you're bringing culture, perspective, and opportunity. But with that comes the pressure to make the right decisions—legally, financially, socially, and academically. You have to understand not just how to play the game, but how to protect your status, your money, and your future.

This book is here to help you do exactly that.

Inside these pages, you'll find answers to questions you didn't even know to ask:

What does my visa allow me to do?

Can I accept NIL deals legally?

How do I report income and avoid tax issues?

What kind of bank or investment accounts can I open in the U.S.?

How do I handle peer pressure, cultural shock, and brand expectations?

We'll also cover what's often left out of NIL conversations—mental health, homesickness, financial scams, faith and identity, and what happens after college. Because NIL is about more than money—it's about **empowerment**, and that means addressing the *whole* student-athlete experience.

Whether you're from Nigeria or New Zealand, Canada or the Caribbean, the Philippines or France, this book was built for you. And whether English is your first language or your fourth, everything inside is written in a way that's clear, direct, and respectful of your journey.

Financial Literacy for NIL – International Student-Athletes Edition is part of a larger educational series designed to support athletes and families at every level. You're not just an addition to that system—you're a priority. The rules may be different for international athletes, but the dream is the same: to leave with more than memories. To leave with options, opportunities, and a future you own.

So take a deep breath. You don't have to figure this out alone. You now have a playbook for the next step of your journey.

Let's begin.

— *Pat Brown, MBA*

Author | Former Division I Athlete | Financial Educator for Athletes Around the World

Quick Note..

Let me be clear right from the jump—I'm not a writer, and I'm definitely not trying to pretend to be one. This book isn't going to follow all the formal rules of grammar, structure, or what some people might call "proper book etiquette." You might catch a typo, a run-on sentence, or something that makes an English teacher cringe.

And you know what? That's okay.

This isn't about being perfect. It's about being real.

I wrote this book because I've got a message that needs to be heard. Too many student-athletes are stepping into a new world of money, deals, and decisions—and they're doing it without the tools they need to succeed. That's why this book exists.

So if the wording gets a little rough or the grammar isn't textbook, I hope you'll give me some grace and stay focused on what matters most: the information, the message, and the mission.

Thanks for reading—and more importantly, thanks for taking your financial future seriously.

How to Use This Book

This book is more than just something to read—it's a resource, a guide, and a playbook designed to walk you through the unique NIL journey as an international student-athlete. Whether you're just beginning to learn about Name, Image, and Likeness (NIL) or already receiving interest from brands or recruiters, this book is here to help you make smart, confident decisions in a system that can be confusing—even for U.S. students.

You don't need to read the entire book in one sitting. In fact, it's written so you can go directly to the chapter that applies to your current situation. Some readers might be most interested in learning how NIL affects visa restrictions, while others may be more focused on taxes, banking, or brand-building. No matter where you begin, you'll find clear explanations, real-world tips, and examples that make complex topics feel a lot more manageable.

You'll also notice that many chapters include reflection questions, checklists, and best practices. These tools are meant to help you take action, not just absorb information. You may want to highlight passages, jot down notes, or create a digital folder to store your NIL-related documents, contracts, and goals. This book is meant to evolve with you—as your opportunities grow, you can return to it again and again for guidance.

It's also important to remember that NIL is a team effort. While you may be the one signing deals and building your name, you're not doing it alone. Share what you're learning in this book with your school's compliance officer, your international student advisor, your family, and anyone else in your support circle. These conversations will help you make smarter decisions and avoid costly mistakes.

Most importantly, don't feel like you need to master everything all at once.

The fact that you're reading this book shows that you're already thinking ahead—and that's what matters most. This book is here to support you step by step, chapter by chapter, as you learn how to manage money, stay compliant, protect your future, and make the most of your NIL experience in the U.S.

So take your time, revisit sections as needed, and use this book as your steady guide through the exciting, sometimes overwhelming, but incredibly rewarding world of NIL.

How This Book Connects to the Full NIL Financial Literacy Series

This book, *Financial Literacy for NIL for International Student-Athletes,* is not a stand-alone manual. It's part of a comprehensive educational series built to support student-athletes and their families at every stage of their NIL journey—from high school through college, from the first NIL opportunity to cross-border career planning and long-term financial freedom.

If you're reading this book, it likely means you've already taken a bold step: you've left home to pursue your academic and athletic dreams in the United States. You're competing in a new country, often in a second or third language, while trying to navigate school, sports, and now—Name, Image, and Likeness. You want to understand how to approach NIL the *right* way—not just to earn a little money, but to protect your visa, your future, and your peace of mind. That's exactly what this book is built to help you do. It's about giving you the knowledge, tools, and systems you need to make informed, confident financial decisions in an unfamiliar environment.

The flagship title in this series, *Financial Literacy for NIL,* is written for college student-athletes managing NIL income in real time. It covers critical topics like budgeting, taxes, credit, contracts, LLCs, investing, and how to protect your brand and reputation. It speaks directly to student-athletes who are already in the middle of the action—signing deals, hiring agents, and learning how to think like entrepreneurs. While that book lays the foundation for navigating NIL as a college athlete, this international edition is designed to walk alongside you as you balance that journey with the **added complexity** of being a non-citizen.

As an international student-athlete, you face unique challenges that domestic athletes often don't think twice about: immigration status, F-1 visa rules, CPT/OPT limitations, double taxation, currency conversion, banking across borders, and cultural adjustments—all while keeping your academic and athletic eligibility intact. *Financial Literacy for NIL for International Student-Athletes* is written to make sure you don't get lost in the system. It's here to protect you from costly mistakes, help you ask the right questions, and empower you to use NIL wisely—without putting your education, status, or long-term goals at risk.

This international edition also ties closely to *Financial Literacy for NIL for High School Student-Athletes,* which is focused on early NIL education—before athletes sign their first deal. That book introduces young athletes to budgeting, branding, decision-making, and long-term planning before the money and pressure hit. Even if you're already competing at the college level, it can be helpful to look back at that foundation, especially if NIL is new to you or you came from a country where financial literacy wasn't taught early.

Finally, this series includes *Financial Literacy for NIL for Parents of Student-Athletes.* That guide is written for the families and guardians of student-athletes, offering them insight into the world of NIL and helping them support their child through it. For international families, this resource can be especially valuable—giving parents a window into what life, money, and opportunity look like for their children studying and competing in the U.S., even from across an ocean or time zone.

Think of these books like your personal NIL team:

- The college edition is your financial playbook.
- The high school edition is your early training ground.
- The parent edition is the headset in the stands—quiet, steady, and supportive.
- And this international edition? This is your compliance officer, cultural interpreter, and global game plan all in one.

No matter where you're from, what your goals are, or what sport you play, this series was built to help you succeed on your terms. You don't have to figure out NIL alone. You don't have to risk your visa or make life-altering mistakes in silence. You've already made the brave choice to leave home and compete at the next level—now it's time to manage your opportunities with confidence.

Because when NIL is done right, it doesn't just change your season.

It can change your future.

And maybe even the future of the family, community, or country you represent.

SECTION I: INTRODUCTION

Welcome to the NIL Era — And Your New Playbook

If you're reading this, congratulations—you're part of something historic.

You're not just a college athlete. You're not just a student. You're an **international student-athlete** navigating a brand-new world where your **Name, Image, and Likeness (NIL)** have real value—and real opportunity.

But there's a catch.

You weren't handed a playbook for how to handle:

- NIL income
- Visa rules
- U.S. banking, credit, and taxes
- Agents and contracts
- Business decisions that could shape your future

And that's where **this guide** comes in.

Why This Book Exists

This book was written because **your experience is different.**

You're not just adjusting to college life—you're adjusting to a **new country, a new culture, and a new financial system.**

You've got dreams of going pro, launching a brand, or helping your family. But you've also got to protect your:

- Student visa
- Athletic eligibility
- Tax and legal status
- Financial future

Nobody told you how to juggle all that.

So now? We're going to figure it out together.

From the Locker Room to Life

Think of this book as your **financial playbook**—designed with international student-athletes in mind.

Whether you're trying to:

- Understand the U.S. financial system
- Learn the dos and don'ts of NIL
- File taxes and protect your visa
- Build a personal brand
- Or just stop living paycheck to paycheck...

You'll find real answers, real strategies, and real examples in the pages ahead.

This isn't written in "finance-speak."

You don't need to be an economics major to get it.

You just need the same mindset you bring to your sport:

Discipline. Curiosity. Hustle.

What You'll Learn in This Guide

- **Visas & Compliance**: What's legal, what's not, and how to protect your status
- **Money 101**: Banking, budgeting, and credit for international athletes
- **NIL & Taxes**: How to earn and report money the right way
- **Brand Building**: How to grow your platform and stand out
- **Business Basics**: Contracts, agents, LLCs, and managing income
- **Long-Term Vision**: Saving, giving back, and building a future beyond sport

Rule of Thumb (Right From the Start):

> ***"If you don't understand it, don't sign it. If you earn it, track it. If you're unsure, ask someone who knows."***

Final Word Before We Begin:

You didn't come this far just to play games.

You came here to **build something bigger**—for yourself, your family, and your future.

So let's get to it.

Let's build your knowledge.

Let's protect your journey.

Let's unlock the full potential of your name, image, and legacy.

Up next: Visas & Compliance—Play by the rules. Stay in the game.

Chapter 1: Why This Book Matters

You're Not Just an Athlete—You're an International Athlete

As an international student-athlete, you've already proven that you're elite. You left your home country, took a leap of faith, and committed to performing—on the field and in the classroom—at the highest level.

That alone is a major accomplishment.

But when it comes to managing money, building credit, paying taxes, or understanding NIL (Name, Image, and Likeness) rules in the United States, your experience is **not the same** as everyone else's.

Your story is different.

And that's exactly why **this book exists**—because financial literacy for international athletes can't be one-size-fits-all.

You Face Unique Challenges with Visas and Legal Limits

Your F-1 visa status comes with serious restrictions that most domestic student-athletes don't even have to think about.

- You can't freely work off-campus
- You may not qualify for certain NIL deals
- You have to report income differently
- Violating visa rules—intentionally or not—can lead to **removal from**

the country

That's not just inconvenient. That's **life-changing**.

This book breaks down what you can (and can't) do with NIL, what "authorized work" really means, and how to protect your status while still exploring financial opportunities that **don't put your future at risk**.

Different Country, Different Money System

You may come from a country where:

- Credit cards aren't common
- Cash is the norm
- Banking systems are heavily restricted or centralized
- Conversations about money happen behind closed doors—or not at all

Now you're in a country where your financial life is expected to be **independent, digital, and credit-based.** You're expected to:

- Open a U.S. bank account
- Understand how to build credit
- File taxes
- Budget with limited income
- Sign contracts
- Evaluate financial offers
- Manage student responsibilities—all while competing in your sport

That's a lot.

This book gives you **clear, step-by-step guidance** so you don't get lost trying to figure out a foreign financial system.

You May Be Far From Home, But Your Financial Foundation Starts Here

Whether you stay in the U.S. after graduation or return to your home country, your time here will leave a **financial footprint**. And the habits you build now will shape your future.

The student-athlete life comes with structure—practice schedules, travel, games, meetings.

But your financial life? That's often left completely up to you.

This book is your **financial playbook**—a guide to help you navigate:

- U.S. banking and budgeting
- International tax rules and treaties
- Safe ways to send money home
- How to avoid scams, fraud, and bad advice
- Legal ways to participate in NIL
- What to look for in agents, advisors, or "friends" who offer to "help"

You Might Be Eligible for NIL (But It's Complicated)

Thanks to new NCAA policies and changes in U.S. law, **NIL is creating real opportunities** for college athletes to earn money while competing. But for international athletes, the path to earning money is filled with legal and logistical landmines.

This book dives into:

- What your visa allows
- When and how you can accept NIL deals
- Workarounds that **don't break the law**
- Ways to **build your brand** now—even if you can't monetize it yet
- How to work with your school's compliance office
- What types of NIL activity might **put your immigration status at risk**

You won't find this explained clearly on social media or in a 30-second TikTok. But you'll find it here—with **your specific situation** in mind.

Financial Mistakes Are Expensive—And Sometimes Irreversible

Some of the most common financial mistakes made by international student-athletes include:

Not knowing you had to file U.S. taxes—even without NIL income

Paying too much to transfer money home

Letting a "friend" sign you up for a shady NIL deal

Using your debit card like a credit card—and draining your account

Ignoring credit or building it the wrong way

Taking advice from someone who "means well" but doesn't understand the system

These aren't just learning moments—they can cause **legal trouble, financial stress, or even impact your ability to stay in the country**.

This book helps you **avoid the landmines** so you can focus on your sport, your studies, and your future.

You Need Advisors Who Understand You

A lot of people will want to offer you advice: teammates, agents, friends, coaches, even strangers online. But here's the truth:

Most people don't understand the **unique intersection** of being a student, athlete, and international guest.

Even fewer know how to explain **money concepts** in a way that actually makes sense for you.

That's why this book doesn't just explain the "what"—it explains the **why**, the **how**, and what it means **for someone in your exact situation**.

Your Financial Future Is Bigger Than College

This book isn't just about surviving college—it's about setting yourself up for success **after** college:

Whether you:

- Go pro
- Work in the U.S.
- Return home
- Or start a business

... the choices you make now **will follow you**.

Your financial literacy—what you know about budgeting, credit, taxes, contracts, and planning—is your foundation. And building it now puts you **miles ahead** of your peers.

Even better? You'll be able to help others back home by leading with knowledge, not fear or confusion.

What This Book Covers (Just for You):

How to open and manage a U.S. bank account

- How credit scores work and how to build one safely
- U.S. tax basics for international students
- What to know about NIL and visa compliance
- How to set up a personal budget (and stick to it)
- Spotting financial scams and red flags
- Understanding student loans and repayment options
- Ways to send money home without high fees
- Building long-term wealth, starting now
- Resources to find trusted advisors and professionals

You Deserve More Than Just a Seat at the Table

You've already overcome language barriers, cultural shifts, homesickness, and academic pressure. Now, you're being asked to make financial decisions that could affect your entire future.

This book exists to say: **You deserve the information. You deserve clarity. You deserve confidence.**

No more guessing. No more vague advice. No more being left out of the conversation.

Let's Build Your Game Plan

This book isn't here to overwhelm you—it's here to walk with you. At your pace. In your language. On your terms.

You don't have to be perfect with money. You just have to be **intentional**.

Because no matter where you're from, **financial freedom starts with financial literacy**.

And yours starts right here.

Chapter 2: Understanding NIL as an International Student-Athlete

In July 2021, the NCAA changed the game forever.

For the first time in history, college athletes in the U.S. were officially allowed to **profit from their Name, Image, and Likeness (NIL)**. That meant you could now get paid for doing things like:

- Endorsing a brand
- Promoting products on social media
- Hosting a sports camp
- Signing autographs
- Appearing in commercials
- Launching your own merch line

For many athletes, this opened the door to **real financial opportunities** during their college careers.

But for international student-athletes?

It opened the door… and then slammed it halfway shut.

Your Visa Status = Your Rules

Most international student-athletes in the U.S. are on an **F-1 visa**, which comes with strict rules about employment. Here's the big difference:

- **Domestic student-athletes** can freely take NIL deals (with some guidance from their schools)
- **International student-athletes** are limited because **F-1 visas restrict employment**

Under F-1 rules:

- You **can't work off campus** without authorization
- You **can't perform services** in exchange for payment without work permission
- NIL is **not explicitly approved or prohibited**, but earning income related to your athletic participation could be interpreted as **unauthorized work**

In short: **You have to be careful. Very careful.**

What Are Schools Doing to Help?

Some universities have stepped up by:

- Offering NIL education programs
- Helping international athletes explore **passive income** opportunities
- Working with immigration attorneys to interpret gray areas
- Partnering with international offices and compliance teams

But there's a catch: **NIL compliance is evolving fast**, and schools are still figuring it out. One school may give you helpful support, while another might offer little clarity at all.

That's why **you have to be your own advocate**—understand the rules, ask questions, and know when to say **no** to a deal that could put your status at risk.

Work vs. Passive Income: What's Allowed?

Let's break down what may or may not be okay:

Type of NIL Activity: Is it Safe for International Athletes?

Paid social media post (U.S.-based)
Risky—may count as unauthorized work

Paid endorsement (filmed in U.S.)
Risky—tied to athletic performance

Selling merchandise online
Maybe—if it's fully passive income

NIL deal completed while home abroad
Safer—if entirely done outside the U.S.

Creating YouTube content (ad revenue)
Maybe—passive if not performance-related

Running a blog or monetized podcast
Depends on content and U.S. activity

Important: Always check with your school's **international student office** and **NIL compliance team** before accepting or promoting anything.

NIL Opportunities: Gender and Sport Breakdown

While opportunities vary across the board, the types of NIL deals—and how athletes benefit—can look very different depending on your **gender** and **sport**.

Female Athletes: Social Media Dominance

- 68% of top NIL earners in NCAA women's sports come from **gymnastics, softball, and volleyball**
- Female athletes are **crushing it** on platforms like TikTok, Instagram, and YouTube
- Many deals focus on **lifestyle, health, fashion, and fitness** brands

Why? Because NIL isn't just about what happens on the field—it's also about your **influence and brand presence**.

Male Athletes: High-Value Sport Deals

- Football and men's basketball dominate the **high-dollar direct endorsement space**
- Larger national and regional sponsorships go toward sports with **TV visibility, ticket sales, and fan engagement**
- The deals may be fewer in number, but they tend to be **higher in value**

So Where Do International Athletes Fit In?

Even if you're not allowed to monetize your NIL in the U.S. yet, you still have **valuable tools at your fingertips**:

Build Your Brand Now

- Grow your social media following
- Create professional highlight reels
- Develop a personal website or digital portfolio
- Engage with your community (without accepting money)
- Position yourself for deals **you can accept later** (like when you return home or secure work authorization)

Go Global

- Consider **doing NIL deals when you're back home** during breaks or summer
- Use international platforms, agencies, or sponsors that align with your home country's rules
- Look into options like **O-1 visas** in the future (for athletes with extraordinary ability)

Real Talk: What Happens If You Violate F-1 Rules?

Violating your visa terms isn't just a slap on the wrist—it can mean:

- **Losing your visa status**
- **Getting barred from reentry**
- **Being removed from your team**
- **Having your scholarship revoked**

You worked too hard to get here. Don't risk it for a few thousand dollars.

Summary: What You Need to Know

- **NIL is allowed in the NCAA**, but your **visa status affects what you can do**
- As an **international student-athlete**, you must avoid activities considered **unauthorized work**
- Always consult your **school's compliance office and immigration advisors**
- Female athletes are excelling in **social media–based NIL**
- Male athletes are landing **higher-value traditional deals**
- Even if you can't get paid now, you can still **build your brand** and **prepare for opportunities later**

Final Word

NIL is new, messy, and powerful. It's changing the lives of athletes across the country—but you can't follow someone else's playbook. Your rules are different. Your path is different.

That's not a disadvantage.

It just means you need the **right information** and a smart strategy.

Let's build it—together.

Chapter 3: Know Your Visa — F-1, CPT, OPT & NIL

When it comes to earning money as an international student-athlete in the United States, your biggest gatekeeper isn't your coach or your performance—it's your **visa.**

And if you don't understand your visa's rules?

You could accidentally put your **education**, your **eligibility**, and your **entire future** at risk.

This chapter breaks down the essentials you **must know** about your **F-1 visa**, what **CPT** and **OPT** mean for you, and how to stay compliant with the rules—especially when it comes to **NIL** opportunities.

What is an F-1 Visa?

The **F-1 visa** is the most common type of student visa used by international student-athletes in the U.S. It's a **nonimmigrant visa** that allows you to:

- Study at a U.S. college or university
- Play college sports
- Stay in the country as long as you're enrolled and making progress toward your degree

But here's the key:

l **It comes with very strict employment restrictions.**

What F-1 Visa Holders Cannot Do:

Unless you've received special permission, **you are not allowed to:**

- Work off-campus
- Accept payment for services performed in the U.S.
- Engage in any form of business or self-employment
- Take NIL deals that involve active work inside the U.S. (e.g., promoting a brand, filming content, signing autographs)

Violation = serious consequences, including:

- Losing your visa
- Being removed from school
- Being disqualified from your athletic program
- Deportation or ineligibility to re-enter the U.S.

What F-1 Visa Holders Can Do (With Conditions):

There are **two main ways** you can earn money legally as an international student while staying compliant:

1. Curricular Practical Training (CPT)

CPT is work authorization that allows you to **gain employment experience related to your major** while still in school.

It must be part of your curriculum or a structured internship program

You must get approval from your school's **Designated School Official (DSO)**

CPT is usually offered **after the first academic year**

Can it apply to NIL?

Possibly, but only if you can prove the NIL activity is:

- Educational in nature
- Tied directly to your course of study
- Approved in advance as part of a CPT program

Example: If you're studying marketing and land an NIL deal that includes analyzing brand performance or campaign strategy **as part of your coursework**, you might qualify for CPT.

2. Optional Practical Training (OPT)

OPT allows F-1 students to work in the U.S. **after graduation** (or in some cases, during school) in a role related to their field of study.

Up to **12 months of work authorization** (can be extended for STEM fields)

NIL income may qualify **if related to your degree field**

You must apply and receive approval from USCIS before working

Example: A communications major who signs an NIL deal to work with a podcast or media brand **after graduating** may be able to use OPT.

Passive Income vs. Active Involvement: Know the Difference

A big part of understanding NIL as an international athlete is knowing the line between **passive income** and **active work**.

Income Type Allowed on F-1 Visa? Examples

Active Income

Usually NOT allowed

Filming paid content, doing brand appearances, social media promotion, autograph signings

Passive Income

Sometimes allowed

Interest from a bank account, stock dividends, royalties, selling digital products you created prior to arriving in the U.S.

Passive = no active work involved once it's set up
Active = requires your time, presence, or performance in the U.S.

Bottom line: If you're **actively doing something for money** in the U.S., and it's not CPT/OPT approved, it's likely a **violation**.

Your Visa = Your Responsibility

Universities can guide you, and advisors can help—but ultimately, **you are responsible** for staying in compliance with your visa.

That means:

- Staying enrolled full-time
- Communicating with your **Designated School Official (DSO)** before starting any new job or NIL opportunity
- Reporting all authorized work
- Avoiding deals that put your status in jeopardy
- Asking questions before making financial commitments

Staying Eligible = Staying in the Game

Violating your visa doesn't just impact your ability to stay in the U.S.—it can:

- Ruin your athletic eligibility
- Damage your academic standing
- Limit your future immigration options
- Affect your chances of going pro, transferring, or working after graduation

You've already made huge sacrifices to be here. Don't let a misunderstanding about NIL and your visa derail everything you've worked for.

Pro Tips for International Student-Athletes:

Ask early – Don't wait until you've been offered a deal. Talk to your school's international office and compliance team **before** you promote, post, or sign anything.

Keep records – Document any NIL conversations, proposals, or content you create—even if you don't get paid. It shows good faith if questions arise later.

Build your brand now – Focus on building your social media presence, personal website, or community connections **without monetizing** (yet).

Use school breaks wisely – You may be able to earn NIL income while visiting home or outside the U.S., depending on how and where the deal is executed.

Don't trust just anyone – Be careful with agents, recruiters, or social media "experts" who don't understand international compliance.

When You Leave the Country...

If you're planning to travel back home over break, that might be a window to **legally complete NIL deals** from outside the U.S.

For example:

- Hosting a virtual Q&A or live stream from your home country
- Signing autographs or doing brand work locally
- Posting NIL-related content while not physically in the U.S.

Pro Tip: Always make sure any income earned abroad is **deposited outside of U.S. bank accounts** and doesn't require physical presence in the States to complete.

Final Thoughts

Your visa isn't just paperwork—it's your **passport to opportunity**. But it comes with boundaries.

As exciting as NIL is, the most powerful thing you can do right now is:

1. Learn the rules
2. Ask the right questions
3. Build your brand legally
4. Stay compliant
5. Plan for your future with intention

Financial freedom starts with financial literacy—especially when you're navigating two systems at once.

Chapter 4: Pros and Cons of NIL for International Athletes

NIL—**Name, Image, and Likeness**—has created exciting new opportunities for college athletes to earn money, build their brands, and gain real-world experience. But if you're an international student-athlete, NIL comes with a **unique set of advantages and challenges**.

This chapter will help you weigh the **real pros and cons** of participating in NIL-related activities so you can make **smart, compliant, and strategic decisions**.

Pros of NIL for International Athletes

Even with the restrictions of an F-1 visa, there are still valuable ways NIL can work *for* you—both now and in the future.

Brand-Building (Global Reach)

Your influence doesn't stop at the U.S. border. As an international athlete, you bring **a global perspective and fan base** that can set you apart in the NIL space.

- You can build a **strong personal brand** that travels with you wherever you go.

- Social media allows you to connect with audiences **in your home country and the U.S.**
- Your international story and background can make you more **marketable** to certain sponsors and followers.

Think long-term: You may not be able to earn now, but building your brand now gives you leverage later—especially if you plan to go pro, return home, or start a business.

Learn U.S. Business Culture

NIL isn't just about money—it's about understanding **how money works** in real-life situations. Even if you can't earn income today, you can still:

- Learn how contracts work
- See how brands evaluate athletes
- Understand marketing, negotiation, and value creation
- Get used to the language of business in the U.S.

This real-world education gives you a **head start**—and it's not something you'll learn in most college classes.

Set the Foundation for Future Sponsorships and Business

You may not be able to **monetize NIL right now**—but you *will* in the future. Whether it's:

- When you go pro
- When you graduate and gain **OPT** status
- Or when you return home and become a major figure in your country

The brand you build during college becomes your **platform for future opportunities.**

Cons of NIL for International Athletes

Unfortunately, it's not all upside. There are serious challenges and risks international athletes must navigate. The consequences of a mistake can be far more severe than for U.S. citizens.

Limited Monetization Options Due to Visa Rules

Your F-1 student visa severely restricts your ability to work in the U.S., including earning money from NIL-related activities.

- You can't sign paid endorsement deals in the U.S. without **specific authorization (like CPT or OPT)**
- You can't appear in ads, monetize your TikTok, or get paid for public appearances unless **very specific conditions are met**
- Even passive income (like online merch sales) can be risky if managed inside the U.S.

Bottom line: **You must be extremely cautious** about how and where you participate in NIL—otherwise, you're risking your entire visa status.

Legal and Immigration Consequences

Violating the terms of your visa—even accidentally—can lead to:

- **Loss of visa status**
- **Expulsion from your school**
- **Ineligibility to compete**
- **Being barred from re-entering the U.S.**
- **Immigration flags** that affect your future career or travel plans

Unlike domestic athletes, you don't get a warning. One wrong move could **shut down your athletic and academic career.**

Complicated Taxes (U.S. and Possibly Your Home Country)

Let's say you *do* find a legal way to earn NIL income (abroad or through CPT/OPT):

- You'll likely owe **U.S. federal and state taxes**
- Your home country might tax that income too, depending on their laws
- You may be subject to **double taxation** unless a tax treaty applies
- You'll need to **file tax returns** and possibly pay **estimated quarterly taxes**

Most U.S.-based tax preparers **don't specialize in international student-athlete tax law**, so you'll need the right help.

Pro Tip: Even if you don't earn NIL income, you may still be required to file IRS Form 8843 each year—just because you're on an F-1 visa.

Quick Comparison: Pros vs. Cons

Pros/ Cons

Global brand-building

Limited earning opportunities

Learn business culture

Strict visa restrictions

Prepares you for the future

Legal and immigration risks

Valuable education

Complicated international taxes

Final Thoughts

Being an international athlete in the NIL era is like playing a game with **a different rulebook**. You can't just copy what your U.S. teammates are doing. What works for them could be a **visa violation** for you.

But that doesn't mean NIL is off-limits.

It means you need a **strategy.** A smart, compliant, long-term game plan.

Use this time to:

- Learn the business side of sports
- Build your digital brand
- Connect with brands and audiences abroad
- Prepare for legal ways to monetize later

Because NIL isn't just about what you can earn now—it's about what you're **building for tomorrow**.

And with the right approach, your story can go global.

SECTION II: Visas & Compliance

Your talent brought you to the U.S.

Your visa lets you stay.

But **breaking even one rule**—even by accident—can risk everything: your scholarship, your eligibility, and your future.

This section breaks down what you **must know** about visas, work rules, NIL participation, and staying fully compliant.

1. Know Your Visa: F-1, CPT, OPT & NIL

Most international student-athletes are on an **F-1 visa**, which comes with **strict employment restrictions.**

F-1 Visa Basics:

- No off-campus work without authorization
- NIL deals in the U.S. often violate visa rules
- On-campus work limited to 20 hours/week during school
- Academic success + full-time enrollment = stay eligible

CPT (Curricular Practical Training)

- Work related to your **major or academic program**
- Requires school and immigration approval
- NIL deals *might* qualify if tied to coursework

OPT (Optional Practical Training)

- Up to 12 months of post-graduation work
- Must be **directly related** to your field of study
- Can be used for NIL work—*if approved*

Always talk to your school's ***international office and compliance team*** *before starting anything.*

2. Work vs. Passive Income

Not all income is treated the same under visa rules.

Type of Income Allowed? Example

Active Work (endorsements, paid posts, events)

Not without CPT/OPT

Paid TikTok ad filmed in the U.S.

Passive Income (royalties, online merch sales)

Maybe (with caution)

Selling designs via Redbubble

Work Done Abroad

Usually allowed

NIL deal completed during summer back home

3. Red Flags That Could Jeopardize Your Visa

Signing a paid NIL deal without checking your visa status

Filming sponsored content on U.S. soil

Getting paid into a U.S. bank account for work done abroad

Letting someone else "use your name" for their business

Not filing the proper tax forms

Always ask before acting. Guessing = risk.

4. Staying Compliant: What You MUST Do

Meet with your **international student advisor** before accepting income
Submit your **Form 8843** every year (even with no income)
File **Form 1040NR** if you earn income
Keep all paperwork: contracts, tax forms, school approvals
Report address changes or visa issues immediately
Check with your **compliance office** for NIL platform approvals

Rule of Thumb:

"Protect your visa like you protect your scholarship."

Because if you lose one, you risk the other.

Final Word

You weren't just recruited for your sport—you were **invited here to succeed.**

And that means **playing by the rules**, not just on the field, but in life.
Stay informed. Ask questions. Build your brand the right way.
You didn't come this far to get sent home for a technicality.

Chapter 5: Budgeting Basics — The "Practice Plan" for Your Wallet

Budgeting = Your Financial Game Plan

Think of budgeting like your team's practice plan or playbook.

If you ignore it, skip reps, or wing it every game—you lose.

But if you **stick to the plan**, run your plays, and make adjustments when needed?

You win.

That's exactly how your budget should work.

It's not there to restrict you—it's there to help you **manage your money**, avoid stress, and stay in control, even when your income changes or your schedule gets wild.

And as a student-athlete, especially an international one, you already have **limited time** and often **limited money**. That's why a simple budget can be a **game-changer**.

The 50/30/20 Rule: A Simple Way to Break Down Your Money

This rule gives you a **clear starting point** for how to divide your monthly income (scholarship stipend, NIL income, job earnings, etc.):

50% → Needs

These are the essentials—stuff you *have* to pay to live, eat, and survive.

30% → Wants

These are your extras. Fun stuff. Things you enjoy, but don't necessarily need.

20% → Savings and Debt

This part goes toward building your future—saving for emergencies, travel, or long-term goals. Also includes paying off any debt.

Let's Break That Down with Examples:

Category / Examples

50% Needs

Food, Rent, Utilities, Phone bill, School supplies, Travel home

30% Wants

Takeout, Games, New sneakers, Haircuts, Concerts, Movies

20% Savings/Debt

Credit card payments, Emergency fund, ✈ Saving for flights, Gifts for family

Rule of Thumb Saying:

> ***"Needs before sneakers. Future before features."***

That means:

- Cover your **basics first**
- Make sure you're saving **before spending on extras**

- You can enjoy your money—but only if you've taken care of what matters most

Your Budget Checklist: Cover the Essentials First

Before you grab those new Jordans or upgrade your iPhone, ask yourself:
"Have I taken care of my essentials this month?"
Here's your **Student-Athlete Budgeting Checklist ⬇**

Monthly Essentials:

- **Food** (groceries, meal prep, occasional eating out)
- **Rent & Housing** (on-campus or off-campus)
- **Utilities** (electricity, water, Wi-Fi if not included in rent)
- **Phone Plan** (talk, text, and data—especially if staying in touch with family abroad)
- **School Costs** (books, materials, software, lab fees)
- **Transportation** (bus, gas, rideshares, bike maintenance)
- **Travel Home** (budget monthly toward flights for breaks or emergencies)

Pro Tip: Don't forget to account for **international transfer fees** or **exchange rates** if you send or receive money from home.

Use the Tools That Work for You

You don't need a complicated spreadsheet or accounting degree to budget. Use whatever helps you **stay consistent**:

- Budgeting apps (like Mint, EveryDollar, YNAB)
- Simple notebook or journal
- Calendar reminders to review your finances weekly
- Keep digital receipts and track spending for a month to see where your money *actually* goes

Budgeting Is a Skill—Just Like Your Sport

Nobody masters their position overnight. It takes **practice, discipline, and coaching.** Same goes for managing your money.

- Budgeting lets you play offense with your finances—not just defense.
- It helps you say "yes" to opportunities and "no" to distractions.
- And it keeps you from falling into traps that leave other athletes broke or stressed out.

Coaches expect you to show up prepared for practice—so do the same for your money.

Final Thought: Budgeting = Freedom

When you have a budget, you don't have to guess.

- You don't have to worry about overdrafting.
- You don't have to call home every time something unexpected comes up.
- You gain **independence. Confidence. Control.**
- And most importantly?
- You make sure your **dreams stay funded.**

Chapter 6: Understanding Credit in the U.S.

If budgeting is your **financial game plan**, then credit is your **reputation in the financial world**.

In the U.S., credit is used for more than just borrowing money. It can affect:

- Whether you can rent an apartment
- Get a car
- Open a phone plan
- Or even qualify for certain jobs

As an international student-athlete, understanding how **credit works**—and how to build it **the right way**—can set you up for success **now and in the future.**

What Is a Credit Score?

A **credit score** is a 3-digit number (usually between **300 and 850**) that shows how trustworthy you are with money.

Here's what it tells lenders:

- Do you pay your bills on time?
- Do you borrow responsibly?
- Do you live within your means?

The higher your score, the better.

Here's a quick breakdown of how scores are usually viewed:

Score RangeWhat It Means

750–850

Excellent

700–749

Good

650–699

Fair

600–649

Poor

Below 600

High Risk

You don't need a perfect score—but you *do* want a **healthy score** to unlock better interest rates and financial options.

How to Build Credit Responsibly

You don't magically get credit—you have to **build it**.

And just like training, you build it through consistent reps over time.

Here's how to get started:

Step 1: Open a Student or Secured Credit Card

If you've never had a credit card before, you may need to start with a:

- **Student credit card** (lower limits, easier approval)
- **Secured credit card** (requires a deposit that acts as your limit)

Example: If you deposit $300 into a secured card, that becomes your credit limit. You use the card, pay it off monthly, and the lender reports your behavior to the credit bureaus.

Step 2: Make Small Purchases (Then Pay in Full)

Use your card for **small recurring items** like:

- Your phone bill
- A weekly meal
- Local transportation

Then—**pay the balance in full** every month.
This builds trust with lenders and helps boost your score over time.

Step 3: Keep Your Utilization Low

Don't max out your credit limit.
A good rule of thumb:

> *Use no more than **30%** of your total credit limit at any time.*

So if your limit is $300, try to keep your balance under $90.

Step 4: Always Pay On Time

This is the #**1 factor** that impacts your credit score.

Set reminders. Automate payments. Use alarms.

Whatever you do—**never miss a due date**.

Even **one late payment** can damage your score.

Avoid the "Buy Now, Cry Later" Trap

Credit cards are not free money.

If you buy more than you can afford and only make **minimum payments**, you'll rack up interest fast.

Let's say you buy $500 worth of gear and only pay $25/month:

- You'll end up paying **hundreds more in interest**
- It could take **years** to pay it off
- Your balance could spiral into long-term debt

That's why it's important to:

- Spend only what you can pay off monthly
- Use credit cards to **build** your future—not **break** it

Pro Tip: If you're tempted to buy something on credit but you wouldn't pay cash for it right now—wait.

Credit Safety Tips for International Athletes

- Use a **U.S.-based bank** that offers student or secured cards
- **Avoid prepaid cards**—they don't build credit
- Monitor your credit with free tools like **Credit Karma** or your bank's app
- Be cautious with apps or "credit repair" companies promising instant

results

- Never co-sign for friends, teammates, or strangers

And remember: **Building credit takes time.**

There's no rush. You're playing the long game.

Final Thoughts

As an international student-athlete, your time in the U.S. may be limited—but your credit history can **follow you for years.**

It can open doors... or slam them shut.

So start small. Stay consistent. And use credit like a tool—not a trap.

Because when used wisely, **credit is a key to freedom—not a chain to debt.**

Chapter 7: Making NIL Work (Legally & Smartly)

By now, you know that **international athletes can't always jump headfirst into NIL deals** like some of your American teammates can. But that doesn't mean you're locked out of the game completely.

There are still smart, strategic ways you can **get involved in NIL—legally and safely.**

This chapter explores how you can make NIL work **for you** through approved school platforms, passive income streams, and brand collaborations that respect your visa limitations.

1. On-Campus NIL Opportunities via School Marketplaces

Many universities have partnered with NIL platforms like:

- **INFLCR**
- **Opendorse**
- **Athliance**
- **Icon Source**

These tools allow you to:

- Create a personal brand profile

- Be discovered by brands
- Manage compliance documents
- Track opportunities (even if you can't accept them yet)

Why it matters:

Even if you can't **take money today**, you can still:

- Build your digital profile
- Get noticed by brands
- Track engagement
- Prep for post-graduation NIL or work authorization periods (like OPT)

Pro Tip: These platforms also help ensure compliance, since they work closely with your school and NCAA guidelines. If you ever **can** monetize, this is one of the safest and cleanest ways to do it.

2. Passive Income Strategies (Play It Safe, Play It Smart)

"Passive income" means you're **earning money without doing active work**—and that's a big deal for F-1 visa holders, because **active work is restricted**.

Here are some **low-risk ways** you can potentially participate in NIL without violating visa rules:

Sell Digital Designs or Merch

If you create:

- T-shirt designs
- Poster prints
- Stickers
- Custom logos or slogans

…you can upload them to platforms like:

- **Redbubble**
- **TeeSpring**
- **Etsy** (if run outside the U.S.)
- **Printful**

These platforms handle sales and shipping—you just collect royalties.

Key Rule: You cannot fulfill orders or run the business manually **inside the U.S.**

But if the platform handles the work? That could fall under passive income.

Royalties from Music or Creative Work

If you've released:

- Music on Spotify or Apple Music
- E-books or courses
- Art or stock photography

…and you're earning **royalties**, that could also qualify as passive income—especially if the content was created **before** you arrived in the U.S. or from abroad.

NFTs & Web3 Products

If you've created **digital art, collectibles, or NFTs**, you might be able to:

- Mint and sell them on platforms like OpenSea or Rarible
- Collect royalty payments on future resales
- Market them to a **global audience** without directly working in the U.S.

Warning: This is still a gray area. Always check with your school's **inter-**

national student office and an immigration attorney before launching NFT-related projects.

3. Collaborate With Approved Brands on Social Media (Carefully)

Social media is one of the **biggest drivers** of NIL deals today. And even if you can't do sponsored posts for pay in the U.S., you can still **prepare your brand and build your following**.

Here's how:

Build Relationships With Brands

Use your platforms (Instagram, TikTok, YouTube, Twitter) to:

- Organically promote brands you love (unpaid)
- Tag companies you want to work with later
- Create content that reflects your lifestyle, sport, or values

This helps you build credibility, even **before** any money changes hands.

Post Strategically While Abroad

Here's where it gets smart:

If you return home over summer break or winter holiday, **you can complete NIL deals abroad** without violating your F-1 visa.

You could:

- Sign a paid sponsorship while outside the U.S.
- Film content at home
- Upload posts during your time abroad
- Receive payment into an international bank account

The key is: **Don't perform the NIL activity physically within the U.S.** unless you're cleared via CPT, OPT, or another legal pathway.

Summary: Smart Ways to Make NIL Work

Strategy Compliant if...
School NIL platforms

You're building your profile, not earning yet
Merch on marketplaces

The platform handles fulfillment (you're not working)
Royalties from music/books

Content created outside the U.S. or before arrival
NFTs and digital art

Sales are automatic and handled outside the U.S.
Social media collaborations

You do the paid work **only while abroad**

Final Word

As an international student-athlete, you have to **play the long game** with NIL.

You might not be cashing checks yet, but you *are* building:

- A brand
- A business foundation
- Real-world experience
- Global visibility
- Future opportunities

Don't rush into something risky. Don't copy what others are doing.

Make NIL work for **you**—legally, smartly, and with vision.

Because your name, image, and likeness aren't just assets...

They're your **legacy.**

SECTION III: Money 101 for International Athletes

You've already proven you belong at the top—in competition, in the classroom, and now... in your finances.

But here's the truth:

No one teaches international athletes how money works in the U.S.—until now.

This section gives you the **financial fundamentals** you *must* understand to succeed off the field, avoid costly mistakes, and build a secure future for yourself and your family back home.

4. U.S. Money vs. Home Country: What's Different?

Being in a new country means adjusting to a **completely different financial system**.

Here's what might be new to you:

U.S. System May Be Different From Home

Credit-based economy

Your country might rely more on cash

Credit cards expected

Debit-only may be more common abroad

File taxes every year

Many countries have automatic systems

Build your own financial history

At home, your family name might carry weight

Independent banking

Parents or sponsors might handle this for you at home

Bottom line: You're responsible for managing it all now—and that means learning the U.S. rules of the money game.

5. Budgeting Basics: The "Practice Plan" for Your Wallet

Budgeting is like your training program—you win when you execute consistently.

Use the 50/30/20 Rule to divide your monthly income:

- **50% Needs**: Food, Rent, Phone
- **30% Wants**: Dining out, Subscriptions, Shopping
- **20% Savings/Debt**: Emergency fund, Credit card payments, ✈ Flights home

Rule of Thumb:

> *"Needs before sneakers. Future before features."*

6. Understanding Credit in the U.S.

Your **credit score** is like your athletic ranking—for your money.

It shows lenders how trustworthy and responsible you are.

Score Range/Meaning

750–850

Excellent

700–749

Good

650–699

Fair

Below 650
Risky

How to build credit:

- Open a **secured or student credit card**
- Spend small, pay off **in full** each month
- **Never miss a payment**
- Keep usage under **30%** of your credit limit

Good credit = better apartment options, car loans, phone plans, and future business deals.

7. Banking in the U.S.

How to open a bank account:

- Choose a student-friendly bank or credit union (low/no fees)
- Bring your passport, I-20, student ID, and proof of address
- Open both:
- **Checking account** for daily use
- **Savings account** for emergency and future funds

Use mobile apps to track spending, set alerts, and avoid overdrafts.

8. Understanding Taxes

Even if you're not earning big NIL money yet—you still may have to **file taxes**.

Form Use
Form 8843
Required if you're on an F-1 visa—even with $0 income
Form 1040NR

File if you earned money in the U.S. (stipends, CPT, etc.)

Need a tax ID? Get an **ITIN** if you're not eligible for a Social Security Number.

Rule of Thumb:

"If you earn, you report. If you guess, you get caught."

9. Avoiding Common Money Mistakes

Don't send all your money home and leave nothing for emergencies

- Don't spend money trying to look rich—focus on **being stable**
- Don't ignore paperwork (visa forms, taxes, banking emails)
- Don't let a teammate or friend handle your money
- Don't assume someone else will "take care of it" for you

10. Tools to Win With Money

- **Budgeting apps**: Mint, EveryDollar, YNAB
- **Credit monitoring**: Credit Karma, Experian
- **Student accounts**: Check with your school's bank partners
- **Advisors**: Your school's international office, compliance team, or a certified financial advisor

Use tech. Use community. Ask questions.

Final Word:

Your talent brought you here—but **your mindset keeps you here**.

Learn how money works.

Master the system.

And start building a future that outlasts your time on the court, field, or track.

This isn't just financial literacy—this is **financial power.**

Up next: **NIL Income—Getting It, Managing It, and Reporting It the Right Way.**

Chapter 8: Taxes & Reporting Income

Let's be honest—nobody gets excited about taxes.

But here's the truth:

If you're an international student-athlete living, studying, or earning money in the U.S., **you have tax responsibilities**—whether you make money from NIL, receive a scholarship stipend, or even work legally through CPT or OPT.

And failing to file correctly? That's a risk you don't want to take.

This chapter breaks down what you need to know about **U.S. tax rules, income reporting, and how to stay compliant** as a non-resident.

Rule of Thumb:

"If you earn, you report—if you guess, you get caught."

U.S. Tax Obligations for Non-Residents

As an international student on an **F-1 visa**, you're considered a **non-resident alien** for tax purposes—at least for your first five calendar years in the U.S.

That means you don't file taxes the same way American citizens or green card holders do.

You file Form 1040NR instead of the standard 1040.

FormUsed By

1040

U.S. citizens and resident aliens

1040NR

Non-resident international students and scholars

You may have to file taxes even if:

- You **didn't earn income** but were present in the U.S.
- You received a **scholarship** that covered living expenses
- You earned **passive income** from abroad that entered the U.S.
- You got paid from a **NIL deal** while overseas but used a U.S. bank account

Important: Even if you didn't earn money, you may still need to submit **IRS Form 8843** every year you're on an F-1 visa.

What Counts as Taxable Income?

- NIL earnings (if allowed under your visa)
- Scholarship money used for **room, board, or travel**
- Wages from approved CPT or OPT
- Royalties or digital product income
- Interest or dividends from U.S. bank accounts (in some cases)

What Doesn't Usually Count (For Taxes)?

- Tuition scholarships or grants
- On-campus housing provided by the school
- Campus meal plans
- Refunds for school expenses

But remember: It all depends on **how the funds are used** and **your country's tax treaty** with the U.S. (if one exists).

Do You Need to Report Foreign Bank Accounts?

Yes—maybe.

If you hold more than **$10,000 USD combined** in foreign accounts (including checking, savings, or investment accounts), you may be required to file a report known as:

FBAR (Foreign Bank Account Report)

- Filed through **FinCEN**, not the IRS
- Required **even if you're not a U.S. citizen**
- Penalties for not filing are **severe**

So if you transfer funds home or keep savings abroad, talk to a tax professional who understands **international tax compliance**.

SSN vs. ITIN: What You Need

To file taxes, you need a tax ID. Here are your two options:

Social Security Number (SSN)

You can get this if you are:

- Approved for on-campus work
- Participating in CPT or OPT
- Receiving taxable NIL income (rare, and only if visa-compliant)

Individual Taxpayer Identification Number (ITIN)

If you don't qualify for an SSN but need to report income or file taxes, you'll apply for an **ITIN** using IRS Form W-7.

This number lets you:

- File a tax return
- Receive refunds (if applicable)
- Stay in good standing with the IRS

Reminder: Filing taxes without the proper ID = automatic red flag.

How and When to File

- **Deadline:** April 15 each year (or the next business day if it falls on a weekend)
- Use services like **Sprintax** (many schools provide access)
- Or hire a tax professional who understands **non-resident returns** and **NIL issues**

What Happens If You Don't File (or File Wrong)?

You could face:

- Fines and penalties
- Loss of visa status
- Denial of future immigration applications (including green cards or work visas)
- IRS audits (yes, they do audit international students!)

This isn't just paperwork. It's about **protecting your ability to stay in the U.S.** and avoid problems that could follow you for years.

Recap: NIL + Taxes for International Student-Athletes

Topic Key Info
Form 1040NR
For non-residents earning U.S. income

Report NIL income
If earned legally, especially via OPT

Report foreign accounts
If over $10,000 USD combined

SSN vs. ITIN
You need one to file taxes

File on time
Or risk penalties and future issues

Final Word

Tax laws may not be exciting, but they are **real—and enforceable.**
And the IRS doesn't care if you didn't "know the rules."
They care that you **followed them**.
So remember:

"If you earn, you report—if you guess, you get caught."

Take the time to understand your obligations, ask your school's international office for guidance, and work with people who know how to file taxes for athletes just like you.

Chapter 9: NIL Branding for International Athletes

You might not be cashing checks from NIL just yet—but you can **absolutely start building your brand** today.

Your **Name, Image, and Likeness (NIL)** is more than just a source of income. It's your personal story. It's your influence. It's your *platform*—and how you use it now can shape opportunities that follow you long after college.

And as an international athlete, you've got something powerful that most of your peers don't:

A global perspective. A unique background. A story worth sharing.

Your Brand Starts With Your Story

Think about it—what makes you *you*?

- You left home to chase a dream in another country
- You speak multiple languages
- You represent your country every time you compete
- You're balancing sport, school, culture shock, and sometimes homesickness

That journey? That's branding gold.

Use your cultural identity to stand out:

- Share stories from home
- Post about how you train, eat, or live differently
- Talk about the values or challenges that shaped you
- Educate and inspire others through your experience

Remember: people follow people—not just stats.

How Male and Female Athletes Use Social Media Differently

Understanding the landscape can help you decide what **type of content** to focus on:

Female Athletes:

- Often excel in **lifestyle, health, fitness, and fashion** content
- Dominate on platforms like **Instagram and TikTok**
- Use aesthetics, consistency, and relatability to build audiences
- More likely to attract **brand partnerships and influencer campaigns**
- **Women's sports NIL is booming**: Gymnastics, volleyball, softball, and track & field are leaders in content-based NIL success

Male Athletes:

- Tend to get higher-value **endorsement and sponsorship deals** (especially in football and basketball)
- Use their platforms to share **highlights, training clips, and motivational content**
- Lean into **performance-based storytelling**
- May be stronger on platforms like **Twitter, YouTube, and Reels**

Pro Tip: No matter your gender, building a consistent, intentional presence online gives you leverage—whether you're selling merch, getting scouted, or launching a business later.

Examples of Smart Branding by International Athletes

Tennis – Coaching Tips via YouTube & Instagram

An international tennis player might:

- Post match highlights with analysis
- Share warm-up routines or footwork drills
- Offer tennis tips for beginners—possibly in their native language
- Show behind-the-scenes travel content from tournaments

Long-form on YouTube + short-form on Reels or TikTok = reach + growth

Soccer – Dual-Language TikToks

A soccer athlete from Spain might:

- Post skill videos with captions in both Spanish and English
- Talk about adapting to the U.S. style of play
- Showcase training differences between their club back home and their NCAA program
- Include reactions or cultural comparisons for entertainment

This strategy widens your audience across borders

Volleyball – Training Guides & Lifestyle Content

A volleyball player from Brazil might:

- Share meal preps or snacks from home

- Talk about staying focused while living abroad
- Post tips for jumping, mobility, or recovery
- Mix athletic content with personality—room tours, playlists, Q&As

Lifestyle content builds connection. Education builds authority.

Tools to Build Your NIL Brand (Even Without Monetizing)

- **Canva** – Create visuals, templates, and digital resumes
- **Linktree** – Add links to all your platforms in one place
- **Instagram Insights / TikTok Analytics** – Track your growth and engagement
- **Personal Website** – Showcase your story, stats, and media all in one place
- **Brand Guide** – Create 3–5 words that describe your content (e.g., "Focused, Global, Relatable")

Final Word

Even if you can't earn NIL income right now, you can absolutely build a **brand worth investing in.**

So don't wait. Show up. Share your journey. Tell your story in your own voice—because the more authentic and intentional you are, the more powerful your platform becomes.

You don't need a sponsorship to have influence.

You just need a story—and the courage to tell it.

Chapter 10: Business Structures & Agents

Let's get one thing straight:

If you're building a brand or earning money through NIL—you're a business.

That might sound wild, especially if you're still balancing class, workouts, and weekend games. But whether you're making $500 or $50,000, you're now dealing with contracts, taxes, negotiations, and branding. That means you need to **think like a business owner**—because that's exactly what you are.

This chapter breaks down:

- How to protect yourself legally
- When (and how) to consider forming an LLC
- What to look for in a trustworthy NIL agent or rep
- And how to avoid getting scammed

LLC Basics: When You're More Than Just a Player

LLC stands for **Limited Liability Company**—a popular business structure used by athletes, freelancers, influencers, and entrepreneurs.

Why set up an LLC?

- **Protects your personal assets** if something goes wrong in a business deal
- Makes it easier to **track income and expenses**
- Gives you a more professional image when negotiating with brands
- Can help with **tax planning** if you start earning significant money

When should you consider forming one?

- You're earning consistent NIL income (now or in the future)
- You're signing contracts with companies or reps
- You're selling merchandise, running a monetized platform, or building a business around your name

Important: **Talk to a tax advisor** and your school's compliance office **before** setting up any business entity. For international students, business ownership may trigger additional immigration concerns or tax responsibilities.

Protecting Yourself in NIL Deals

Here's the truth: once you start building a brand, **people will want a piece of it**—some helpful, some shady.

You've got to know how to **protect your Name, Image, and Likeness (NIL)** before signing anything.

Always:

- **Read every contract**—or have someone who knows what they're doing read it for you
- Ask: What are they getting from you? What are you getting in return?
- Look for **start and end dates**, **payment terms**, and **usage rights**
- Clarify what happens if either party wants to end the deal

Never:

- Sign a deal without reading it
- Agree to give away your **name, image, or brand rights** permanently
- Let someone pressure you to "hurry up and sign"
- Agree to pay large upfront fees without proof of service

Choosing the Right Agent or NIL Rep

If someone wants to represent you—**make sure they're legit.** A good agent or NIL rep should help you:

- Understand and negotiate contracts
- Build your brand
- Manage communication with sponsors
- Ensure legal and tax compliance
- Align with your personal and professional goals

What to Look For:

Green Flags Red Flags

- Licensed or registered
- No website, no reviews, no references
- Experience with student-athletes
- Promises "guaranteed" deals
- Transparent fee structure
- Takes a % before you make money
- Understands NCAA/international rules
- Pushes you to hide income or cut corners
- Encourages long-term planning
- Only talks short-term cash

Ask other athletes about their experiences—and trust your gut.

Rule of Thumb:

"If it sounds too good, it's probably too shady."

- If someone promises you a massive deal right away with no effort or paperwork?
- If they ask for money upfront before showing results?
- If they say, "Don't worry about your visa or taxes"?
- You've worked too hard to let someone mess up your eligibility, your reputation, or your future.

Final Word

Branding yourself means **owning your power**, not giving it away.

Whether you're thinking about NIL today or building for tomorrow, you have the right to:

- Know your worth
- Protect your name
- Build a business that aligns with your values
- Surround yourself with people who have your back, not their hand in your wallet

Don't let fear or pressure lead to bad decisions.

Build slowly. Learn constantly. Ask questions.

Because this isn't just NIL—it's the foundation of your **financial legacy.**

Chapter 11: International NIL Readiness Checklist

Before you dive into NIL or build your brand in the U.S., you need to have your **legal, financial, and strategic foundation** in place. As an international student-athlete, the rules are different—but with preparation, you can still thrive.

Use this checklist as your **NIL game-day prep**.

International NIL Readiness Checklist

Task

Know your visa status (F-1, CPT, OPT, etc.) and what's allowed under immigration law

Set up a U.S. bank account (for managing income, saving, and tracking expenses)

Create a monthly budget using the 50/30/20 rule to control your cash flow

Get a tax ID number (ITIN) if you're not eligible for a Social Security Number

Know your school's NIL rules and talk to compliance and international student services

Understand tax filing requirements (Form 1040NR, FBAR, and IRS deadlines)

Build a personal brand strategy (platform, tone, visuals, and goals)

Follow trusted NIL professionals (agents, attorneys, advisors, and mentors)

Track NIL income & expenses (use spreadsheets, apps, or an accountant if needed)

Bonus Tips:

- Review this checklist every semester and before school breaks
- Keep a physical or digital folder with all documents: visa copies, tax forms, contracts, and brand deals
- Bookmark your school's NIL platform and IRS tax resources
- Ask for help—there's no shame in getting advice from people who've been there

Final Word

Being NIL-ready isn't just about being eligible—it's about being **empowered**.

This checklist gives you the **confidence, structure, and strategy** to move forward legally, ethically, and intentionally as you build your brand and your future.

Stay prepared
Stay compliant
Stay focused

You've already beat the odds to be here. Now it's time to **level up—on your terms.**

Chapter 12: Understanding Currency Exchange and International Banking

"Your hustle is global—your money should move just as smart."

As an international student-athlete, your financial situation is unique. You may be receiving NIL payments, part-time income, or scholarships in U.S. dollars—but your family, savings goals, or responsibilities might be tied to your home country's currency. That means every dollar you move between countries comes with **exchange rates, hidden fees, and timing decisions** that can make or break your money.

In this chapter, we'll help you **master your global finances**—so you can manage your U.S. account, send money home safely, and avoid getting crushed by fees or poor currency decisions.

Managing Money Between the U.S. and Your Home Country

U.S.-Based Bank Account

You'll need a U.S. account to:

- Receive NIL payments or stipends

- Pay for food, rent, transportation, and bills
- Track income for taxes

Tip: Use banks with low fees and mobile access, like Chase, Capital One, Bank of America, or your school's credit union.

Home Country Account

Keep your home account to:

- Send or receive money from family
- Convert U.S. dollars into your local currency
- Pay bills back home or save in local currency

Tip: Know your home country's rules around international transfers, currency conversion, and account limits.

Currency Exchange Fees: The Hidden Cost

Every time you move money between currencies, someone is making money off of you. Most people don't even realize **how much they're losing**.

Common Fees:

- **Markup on exchange rates** (usually 1–3%)
- **Flat wire transfer fees** ($10–$50)
- **ATM withdrawal fees** abroad (1–3%)
- **Receiving fees** at your home bank
- **Dynamic Currency Conversion (DCC)** when using your card internationally

Example:

If the real rate is $1 = 100 pesos, and your provider gives you $1 = 97 pesos, you're losing 3%—that's **3,000 pesos** on every $1,000 you send home.

How to Reduce Currency Exchange Fees

Use Fintech Apps Instead of Banks

Apps like **Wise**, **Revolut**, **Remitly**, and **PaySend** offer better rates and lower fees than traditional banks.

App Best For Speed Fees

Wise

Transparent fees, mid-market rates

1–2 days

0.5–1.5%

Revolut

Multi-currency wallets

Instant to 2 days

Free to low

Remitly

Sending to family

Same day–3 days

Low

PaySend

Flat-fee transfers

1–2 days

$2–$5

Western Union

Cash pickup (only when needed)

Same day

High

Tip: Use Monito.com to compare services and find the cheapest option.

Send Fewer, Larger Transfers

- Instead of sending $100 weekly, send $400 monthly
- Most services charge **per transaction**, so you save by batching

Avoid Dynamic Currency Conversion

- When using your U.S. card abroad, **always choose to pay in the local currency**
- Let your bank convert—it's almost always cheaper

Use Multi-Currency Accounts

Platforms like Revolut let you hold multiple currencies, so you can convert at **the best time**, not just when you're forced to.

Understanding Currency Fluctuations

Exchange rates change daily due to global markets. A strong dollar one day may become a weak dollar the next.

Watch for:

- Political changes in either country
- Economic news or inflation rates
- Timing around holidays and weekends

Tip: Set up **rate alerts** in Wise or Revolut so you know when it's a good time to send money.

When and How to Send Money Home Safely

Step-by-Step:

1. **Decide the amount and urgency**
2. **Compare providers and fees**
3. **Double-check recipient details**
4. **Send during business hours** for faster processing
5. **Track your transfer** until it's confirmed

Security Tip: Never send through unverified apps or use someone else's account—it can raise red flags and delay your money.

Choosing the Right Apps and Services

Here's a quick guide to common tools for sending money internationally:

Service Strength Watch Out For

Wise

Best rates, transparent

Can take 1–2 days

Revolut

Budget-friendly, multi-currency

Less global reach

Remitly

Great for family support

Fees for speed options

Western Union

Cash pickup in rural areas

High fees and markups

PayPal/Xoom

Easy but expensive

High fees and slow for big transfers

Pro Tip: Use Wise or Revolut for most of your transfers. Use Western Union only if your family has no bank access.

Common Mistakes to Avoid

Sending money without checking the exchange rate

- Using your bank for transfers without comparing fees
- Letting someone else manage your money
- Rushing transfers out of emotion or pressure
- Ignoring the taxes and reporting requirements for large transfers

Build Your Global Banking Strategy

Here's your simple action plan:

1. Open and use a U.S. bank account for everyday income
2. Keep your home account for long-term family needs
3. Use **Wise or Revolut** for transfers, not your bank
4. Track all transfers in a spreadsheet or app
5. Set up rate alerts and batch your transfers

Remember: The smartest athlete isn't just focused on performance—they're focused on protection.

Final Word: You're a Global Athlete—Act Like a Global Earner

You don't just play internationally—you live, earn, and move like an international professional. That means mastering your money **across borders**, not just within one account.

Smart currency exchange isn't about luck—it's about **timing, tools, and knowledge**. If you learn to manage this now, you'll save thousands over your lifetime, reduce stress, and set your family and yourself up for long-term stability.

You deserve to **keep more of what you earn**—and now, you know how.

SECTION IV: NIL Income — Getting It, Managing It, Reporting It

You've worked hard to build your brand and represent your sport—but now comes the real test:

What do you do when money starts coming in?

This section walks you through how to **legally earn NIL income**, **manage it wisely**, and **stay compliant** with tax and visa rules—so you can protect your future while building wealth today.

Let's break it down step by step.

6. Understanding Credit in the U.S.

- **What's a credit score?** A 3-digit number that shows how responsible you are with money
- **Why it matters:** Needed for renting, phone plans, cars, or even pro contracts
- **How to build it:**
- Open a **student or secured credit card**
- Make small purchases and **pay in full each month**
- Keep credit usage below 30% of your limit
- **Never miss a payment**

Watch out: Don't fall into the "buy now, cry later" trap. Use credit to build your future—not fake your lifestyle.

7. Making NIL Work (Legally & Smartly)

- Use **school NIL platforms** like Opendorse or INFLCR to connect with approved brands
- Focus on **passive income** (royalties, online products, digital art, global sales)
- Do NIL deals **while home abroad** when permitted by your visa
- Build your brand now—even if you can't legally monetize yet

Stay proactive, but never rush into a deal that puts your visa or reputation at risk.

8. Taxes & Reporting Income

- F-1 visa holders must file **Form 1040NR** (non-resident tax return)
- May also need to file **Form 8843** (even if you earned nothing)
- You might owe U.S. taxes on NIL income—**and possibly in your home country too**
- Got more than $10K abroad? You may need to file **FBAR** (Foreign Bank Account Report)
- Need a **Social Security Number (SSN)** or **ITIN** to file taxes

Rule of Thumb:

> ***"If you earn, you report—if you guess, you get caught."***

9. NIL Branding for International Athletes

- Use your **story, heritage, and language** as branding strengths
- Target both U.S. and global audiences
- Choose your platforms wisely (e.g., Instagram, TikTok, YouTube, Twitter)
- Share a mix of:

- Training content
- Lifestyle moments
- Tips or behind-the-scenes from your unique perspective

Remember: Your influence starts with your identity. Be real, be you, and stay consistent.

10. Business Structures & Agents

- Learn the basics of forming an **LLC** (later, when legally allowed)
- Be cautious with agents and reps—ask for credentials, references, and a clear payment structure
- Don't sign anything you don't understand—consult school compliance, an attorney, or a trusted advisor

Rule of Thumb:

> ***"If it sounds too good, it's probably too shady."***

Recap: Your NIL Income Game Plan

Step What to Do

1. Learn your visa limits—don't guess what's legal
2. Set up a **U.S. bank account** and track all earnings
3. Start building **credit responsibly**
4. Explore **passive and compliant NIL income options**
5. File taxes **correctly and on time**
6. Work with trusted advisors, not random "agents"

Final Word:

Getting money is exciting. Keeping it is powerful. Reporting it is non-negotiable.

You have a unique path as an international student-athlete.
With the right strategy, support, and mindset, you can:

- Earn smart
- Manage wisely
- Stay eligible
- And prepare for life after college with **real financial confidence**

Chapter 13: Social Media Safety, Sponsorship Etiquette, and Cultural Awareness

"Your platform is powerful. Use it wisely."

As an international student-athlete, your story, image, and voice carry weight. You're not just representing your school or your sport—you're often representing an entire country, culture, or region. In the NIL era, your online presence isn't just for fun—it's part of your brand, your business, and your reputation.

This chapter is your guide to **staying safe, staying professional, and staying respected** while navigating sponsorships, cultural sensitivity, and the ever-watching world of social media.

Social Media Safety: Protecting Your Brand and Identity

Your social media accounts are an extension of you. If you're not intentional, a single post can damage your reputation, your eligibility, or even your visa status.

Do:

- Use two-factor authentication to secure your accounts
- Regularly review your privacy settings
- Keep personal location sharing OFF
- Be selective with what you post—it never really disappears

Don't:

- Post during emotional moments—pause before you post
- Share too much personal or family information publicly
- Join viral trends without understanding their meaning
- Engage with trolls or argue publicly online

Rule of Thumb: If you wouldn't want your coach, your school, or your family seeing it—don't post it.

Cultural Awareness in a Global Space

As an international athlete in the U.S., you're interacting with a wide range of people and perspectives. What's considered funny, cool, or acceptable in your country **may be misunderstood** or offensive in another.

Examples of Cultural Missteps:

- Gestures or slang that mean different things in the U.S.
- Posting political or religious opinions without context
- Using humor or memes that don't translate across cultures
- Assuming followers understand your background or language

Tips for Staying Culturally Aware:

- Research U.S. cultural norms before posting or reacting
- Avoid generalizations or stereotypes
- Follow and observe how other successful international athletes present themselves online
- When in doubt, ask a trusted teammate, mentor, or coach for feedback

Turning Cultural Identity Into Brand Strength

Your cultural background is a **superpower**—when used thoughtfully.

Athletes from different regions often attract unique attention and fanbases because of their language, traditions, or backstories. Sharing where you're from can help people connect with you—**but how you share it matters**.

Smart Ways to Showcase Your Culture:

- Share food, family traditions, or celebrations
- Use dual-language captions or subtitles
- Highlight your journey and what makes it special
- Partner with brands that support cultural diversity
- *Your story is your edge—just present it with pride and professionalism.*
- Sponsorship Etiquette: Communicating With Brands and Reps

If you're building a brand or being approached for sponsorships, how you respond matters just as much as your athletic ability.

Professional Communication Tips:

- Always respond to emails/messages with gratitude and clarity
- Use complete sentences, proper punctuation, and respectful tone
- Keep your bio, email, and links updated on all social platforms
- If you need help reviewing a contract, ask your coach, school advisor,

or a legal expert

Sample Email Response:

Hi [Brand Name],

Thank you for reaching out! I'm honored you're interested in working together. I'd love to learn more about your campaign and how I can be involved. Please feel free to send over details and next steps. Looking forward to hearing from you!

Best, [Your Name]

Dealing With Trolls, Scams, and Reputation Risks

Not everyone online has good intentions. With your visibility comes a higher risk of being **targeted or misrepresented**.

Scams to Watch For:

Fake agents offering you "guaranteed deals"

Phishing messages pretending to be brands or schools

People asking for your login info, SSN, or bank account

"Collab" offers with shady links or unusual payment requests

How to Stay Protected:

Never sign or agree to anything without doing research

Block and report suspicious accounts immediately

Keep all NIL or sponsorship conversations in writing

If something seems too good to be true—it probably is

Your reputation is worth more than a quick deal. Protect it like you protect your name on the back of your jersey.

Mistakes Happen—Here's How to Recover

If you accidentally post something that causes backlash or misunderstanding:

Take it down immediately

Reflect—what was the intent vs. the impact?

Apologize if necessary—brief, sincere, and to the point

Don't get defensive or argue in the comments

Learn from it and be more thoughtful going forward

Being proactive and honest about mistakes earns more respect than pretending they didn't happen.

Final Word: Post With Purpose

You don't need a huge following to have a powerful presence.

Every post, every share, and every comment is part of your **digital resume**.

And in today's world, that resume travels faster and further than anything else.

So be smart. Be intentional. And be proud of who you are—on and off the screen.

Because your story is global. Your brand is growing. And your voice matters.

Chapter 14: NIL and Education – Balancing Academics, Athletics, and Income

"You're more than a student. More than an athlete. You're a full-time brand, balancing books, balls, and business."

For international student-athletes and domestic ones alike, the NIL era has brought exciting opportunities—but also new pressures. Suddenly, you're expected to juggle **class schedules, practices, game film, conditioning, sponsorship deadlines, social media content**, and maybe even brand partnerships or side hustles.

It's a lot.

And if you're not careful, your education—the very thing that brought you to the U.S.—can take a back seat.

This chapter is here to help you stay grounded. Because your NIL is valuable—but **your education is priceless**.

Why Your Degree Still Matters

No matter how big your NIL earnings get, your education is still:

- Your **ticket to a long-term career**
- Your **protection** against injury or setbacks

- Your **path to opportunities** beyond athletics

If you're an international student, staying enrolled full-time and in good academic standing is **not optional**—it's a condition of your visa. If your grades slip or you drop below full-time status, you could lose your student visa and, with it, your chance to stay in the U.S.

Time Management Tips for a Full Plate

When you're managing NIL work, school, and your sport, time becomes your most valuable resource. Use it wisely.

Strategies That Work:

- **Use time blocking:** Schedule specific hours for class, homework, brand work, and rest. Stick to it.
- **Create a weekly priority list:** What must get done? What can wait?
- **Set social media hours:** NIL doesn't need to dominate your day.
- **Have a "shutdown" time:** At some point every day, shut off and recharge.

Tools to Keep You Organized:

- Google Calendar or iCal (sync with class and team schedules)
- Notion, Trello, or ClickUp (for to-do lists and content planning)
- Alarmed or Reminders app (to set mini deadlines or study breaks)
- Physical planners or whiteboards (visual reminders for visual learners)

Setting Academic Goals

Set short-term and long-term academic goals just like you set athletic ones.

- **Short-Term:** "I will complete every reading before class this week."

- **Mid-Term:** "I want a 3.2 GPA this semester."
- **Long-Term:** "I will graduate with honors in my major."

Talk to your **academic advisor** about workload balance, elective choices, and tutoring services. There's no shame in asking for help—especially when your plate is this full.

When NIL Becomes a Distraction

The truth? NIL can be overwhelming. When there's money coming in, social media expectations rising, and brands watching, it's easy to lose focus on your coursework.

Signs NIL is starting to hurt your education:

- You're skipping class to film content
- Your assignments are late or rushed
- You're studying less than before NIL started
- You feel burned out or constantly anxious

What to Do:

1. **Step back and reassess:** Is this deal or opportunity really worth it?
2. **Talk to a mentor, coach, or advisor:** Let them help you reset priorities.
3. **Streamline your brand obligations:** Not all partnerships are worth your peace.
4. **Set clear boundaries:** NIL work happens outside of class/study time.

International Student-Athletes: Protecting Your Visa

If you're on an F-1 visa, the stakes are even higher. You must:

- Maintain **full-time enrollment** (usually 12 credit hours or more)
- Make **satisfactory academic progress**
- Stay within the guidelines for **work eligibility**

NIL income is **not a free pass**. One academic misstep can lead to a **visa violation**, which puts your scholarship, your degree, and your ability to remain in the U.S. at risk.

Tip: Always work with your school's **international student office** and **compliance team** before committing to any NIL-related opportunity that may impact your academic standing or visa status.

Communicate With Your Team

The best athletes know how to communicate. Don't try to handle this all in silence.

Let your:

- Professors know your schedule (and respect their time)
- Coaches know when you're feeling overwhelmed
- Brand partners know your priorities (student > athlete > brand)
- Family and friends support you without distracting you

Creating an honest support system can be the difference between balance and burnout.

Sample Weekly Time Block (Just a Framework)

Time Task

7:00–8:00 AM

Workout / Conditioning

8:00–9:30 AM

Breakfast + Class 1

10:00–11:30 AM

Class 2

12:00–1:00 PM

Study Hall / Homework

1:00–3:00 PM

Practice / Rehab

3:30–4:30 PM

NIL content planning / brand check-ins

5:00–6:00 PM

Dinner + Relaxation

6:30–8:00 PM

Homework or Group Project Work

8:00–9:00 PM

Downtime / Free time

9:30 PM

Lights out or calm activity

Customize it based on your schedule—but build in breathing room.

Education Is the Greatest NIL of All

NIL income is powerful. But your education is what will pay you **forever**—in opportunities, in access, and in confidence.

Don't let short-term sponsorships or social media shine distract you from graduating with purpose. Whether you go pro or not, your degree is the one thing no one can take from you.

Key Reminders

- **Prioritize class the same way you prioritize training.**
- **Ask for help before things fall apart.**
- **Say "no" to NIL opportunities that hurt your academic goals.**
- **Remember: NIL is an opportunity, not a requirement.**
- **Your brain is your best brand.**

Final Word: Stay Ready, Stay Balanced

You are capable of achieving all three: **Education. Athletics. Income.**

But it will take effort, intention, and structure. The NIL era is exciting—but it's not worth sacrificing your long-term potential for short-term paychecks.

Your best NIL deal is graduating with purpose, clarity, and the tools to build a legacy far beyond the field.

Stay focused. Stay enrolled. Stay winning.

Chapter 15: Networking in the NIL Era – Relationships That Build Your Future

"Your next opportunity might not come from your performance—it might come from a conversation."

NIL is about more than money. It's about access. Visibility. And most importantly—**relationships**. As a student-athlete in the NIL era, you're not just building a brand—you're building a **network** that can shape your life beyond the game.

This chapter will show you how to **build relationships the right way**, use platforms like LinkedIn to your advantage, and turn NIL moments into **meaningful mentorships, internships, and long-term opportunities.**

Why Networking Matters—Especially in the U.S.

In the U.S., **who you know** often matters just as much as what you know. Relationships can lead to:

- Job offers
- Brand deals
- Mentorships
- Speaking engagements
- Life advice

For international student-athletes, building these relationships can also mean:

- Expanding your visa options post-graduation
- Accessing career paths you didn't know were open to you
- Developing a community when you're far from home

Networking isn't about being fake. It's about being present, respectful, and ready.

Who Should Be in Your Network?

Here are key people worth connecting with now—not later:

Professors & Faculty

- They can write recommendation letters, refer you for grad programs, or connect you with their own professional contacts.
- Show up, ask good questions, and attend office hours.

Alumni

- Former athletes or students who've "been there, done that."
- Check if your school has an **alumni mentorship program** or LinkedIn group.

Local Business Owners

- Especially those who support your team or sponsor athletes.
- Can lead to NIL deals, internships, or job shadowing opportunities.

Brand Reps from NIL Events

- Don't just take the free merch—talk to the people behind the table.
- Ask them how they got started, what they look for in athlete partnerships, and how to stay in touch.

Former Coaches, Trainers, and Teammates

- These are long-term allies who understand your journey.
- Great for career support and emotional guidance.

LinkedIn: Your Off-the-Field Highlight Reel

LinkedIn is your **professional social media**—and it's one of the most underused tools by student-athletes.

Why You Need It:

- Shows sponsors, schools, or employers what you're about
- Documents your NIL work, speaking engagements, and internships
- Keeps you connected even after graduation

Quick Setup Guide:

- **Profile Picture**: Use a clear, professional headshot (your jersey is okay!)
- **Headline**: Example – *Student-Athlete | NIL Brand Partner | Business Major at [Your School]*
- **About Section**: Write 3–4 sentences about your story, goals, and passion
- **Experience**: List your athletic achievements, NIL deals, internships, volunteer work
- **Skills**: Include things like leadership, time management, branding, communication

- **Connect**: Start by adding teammates, classmates, professors, coaches, and family

LinkedIn is your digital resume—keep it clean, updated, and focused.

Following Up After Events and Meetings

Networking doesn't stop when the event ends—it begins there.

After an NIL event, speaking engagement, or meeting:

1. **Get their name and contact info** (email, LinkedIn, Instagram)
2. **Send a message within 24–48 hours**
3. Example:

   Hi [Name], it was great meeting you at [Event]. I really enjoyed hearing about [Topic]. I'd love to stay connected and learn more about your work in [Industry]. Wishing you continued success!

1. **Engage occasionally**: Like their posts, comment thoughtfully, share their work when appropriate

Be consistent, but not pushy. Networking is a marathon, not a sprint.

Turning NIL Into Long-Term Opportunities

NIL isn't just about making money—it's about building a **professional reputation**.

If you handle your brand deals the right way:

- Be on time
- Communicate clearly
- Deliver what you promised (content, event appearances, etc.)

- Say thank you—and stay in touch

You'll stand out as someone who is **trustworthy, coachable, and business-minded**. That's exactly who brands and companies want on their teams long-term.

NIL Career Opportunities:

- A fitness brand may offer you a post-grad ambassador role
- A media company might want to hire you for content creation
- A donor or sponsor may refer you to a paid internship
- A business leader may become your long-term mentor

Always think long-term: "How can this opportunity open the next door?"

Where to Start If You're New to Networking

- Attend NIL workshops, alumni mixers, or speaker events at your school
- Practice introducing yourself: who you are, what you do, what you're interested in
- Reach out to one new person each month and ask for a 15-minute conversation
- Join a student organization or business club to expand your network

Example Elevator Pitch:

> *"Hi, my name is [Your Name]. I'm an international student-athlete from [Country], playing [Sport] at [School]. I'm currently majoring in [Major] and building my brand through NIL work focused on [Area—fitness, culture, storytelling]. I'm passionate about learning more about [Industry], and I'd love to connect!"*

Final Word: Your Network is Your Net Worth

Opportunities often come from conversations. From connections. From being in the right place at the right time—and being **ready**.

So don't wait until your career is over to build relationships that matter.

Start now.

Be curious.

Be consistent.

And always bring value to the people you meet.

Because your NIL might start with Instagram—but your future will grow with **LinkedIn, lunch meetings, and long-term partnerships.**

Chapter 16: Life After College – What Happens to Your NIL and Visa?

"The game may change, but your future is still in play."

Graduation is an exciting milestone—but for international student-athletes, it can also raise tough questions:

- What happens to your visa?
- Can you still earn from NIL?
- Do you have to go home?
- What if you want to stay and build a business?

This chapter is all about preparing for life after college—not just from an academic standpoint, but from a **legal, financial, and brand perspective**. Whether you're looking to stay in the U.S. or return to your home country, your next moves should be intentional, strategic, and informed.

What Happens to Your NIL After Graduation?

The short answer: **It depends.**

If you're still in the U.S. and have legal work authorization (like OPT), you can continue building your NIL brand, sign sponsorship deals, or even create a business.

However:

- If your visa expires and you're not authorized to work, NIL earnings **could violate immigration laws**
- You must be **careful about passive vs. active income**, especially as it relates to your visa type

Tip: Always consult with your school's international student office or an immigration attorney before continuing NIL activity after graduation.

Understanding OPT (Optional Practical Training)

OPT is one of the **most important tools** international students have after graduation. It gives you **up to 12 months** to work in the U.S. in a job **related to your major**.

What You Can Do on OPT:

- Work full-time in a professional setting (internships, full-time jobs)
- Work for a business or brand related to your field of study
- Continue building your personal brand **if it ties to your academic focus** (e.g., marketing, business, media)

What You Can't Do:

- Freelance or do unrelated side gigs (e.g., driving for Uber, personal training, etc.)
- Accept NIL offers that aren't connected to your OPT-approved employment
- Stay in the U.S. past your grace period without changing visa status

If your NIL activity qualifies as work aligned with your degree (e.g., digital marketing, entrepreneurship, branding), you may be able to continue—but only if it's documented and approved.

Using Your NIL Brand to Launch a Career

You may not go pro as an athlete—but you can go pro in life.

Your NIL brand is a **launch pad**. Sponsors, content creation, social media, public speaking—these can lead to:

- Marketing jobs
- Media and brand strategy roles
- Speaking and consulting gigs
- Entrepreneurship and business building

Your NIL experience is valuable real-world experience—make sure it's on your resume, LinkedIn, and in your post-grad interviews.

If You're Returning Home: Make Your NIL Global

Going back to your home country? That doesn't mean your brand disappears.

Here's how to bring it with you:

Global Brand Strategies:

- Continue content creation with a **dual-language approach**
- Partner with **regional sponsors** or global companies in your market
- Launch an online coaching, training, or branding business in your country
- Host camps, clinics, or events tied to your U.S. experience

Your journey from your home country to the U.S. and back is inspiring—lean into it.

What About Taxes?

If you earned money through NIL in the U.S., you've likely already filed U.S. taxes. But when you return home, things may change.

Questions to Ask a Tax Advisor:

- Do I need to report U.S. earnings in my home country?
- Am I taxed again on NIL income I earned in the U.S.?
- If I start a business abroad, how should it be structured?

Tax laws vary widely by country. Seek advice from a cross-border tax professional or accountant before making any large moves with your NIL earnings.

Planning Your Exit: Be Proactive

Don't wait until your last semester to figure out what's next. Here's a checklist to help you prepare:

Post-Graduation Planning Checklist:

Meet with your international student advisor about OPT

- Apply for OPT early (usually 90 days before graduation)
- Build or update your resume and LinkedIn profile
- Talk to your professors about job or internship connections
- Reach out to sponsors or mentors for potential opportunities
- Research visa options if you want to stay longer (e.g., H-1B, O-1, entrepreneurship visas)
- Make a financial plan for returning home (saving, transferring funds, exchange rates)
- Archive your content, contracts, and NIL documents for your portfolio
- Consider launching a remote-friendly or global brand model

Real Talk: Don't Panic, Plan

It's normal to feel overwhelmed about what happens next. But you've already done something incredible—you've competed at a high level, built a personal brand, and managed academics in a foreign country. That's not luck—that's **grit, adaptability, and focus**.

Whether you stay in the U.S. or go back home, you're not starting from zero.

You're launching from experience.

Final Word: NIL is Just the Beginning

Your time in college was about more than your sport. You learned how to compete, how to create, how to lead—and how to hustle.

As your student visa expires and your NIL chapter closes (at least in its current form), remember: **you're not losing your opportunity. You're evolving it.**

Build a future that aligns with your values, your skills, and your vision—wherever in the world you land.

Because NIL may have started during school—but the name, image, and legacy you build next...

That's for life.

SECTION V: Building Your Brand & Business Acumen

Your skills on the field brought you here.

Your story and identity? That's what will **set you apart** in the world of NIL.

In this section, you'll learn how to:

- Build an authentic and marketable personal brand
- Understand your value beyond your sport
- Develop basic business skills for managing your NIL success
- Create opportunities that align with your goals and your values

Remember: you're not just an athlete—you're a **personal brand**, a **business**, and a **role model**.

9. NIL Branding for International Athletes

- **Tell Your Story**: Use your cultural background, language, and journey to connect with global audiences
- **Different Platforms, Different Purposes**: Use Instagram for visuals, TikTok for fun, Twitter for thought leadership, YouTube for deeper engagement
- **Examples**:
- Tennis: Share coaching tips, gear reviews

- Soccer: Post dual-language highlights and lifestyle content
- Volleyball: Use Instagram/TikTok for fan engagement and behind-the-scenes access

Key Message: Your brand is your voice. Be real. Be consistent. Be global.

10. Business Structures & Agents

- **LLC 101**: Know what an LLC is, and when it makes sense to form one (once you legally can earn)
- **Working With Agents**:
- Look for transparency, experience, and NCAA/international rule knowledge
- Don't rush—interview them like you would a coach
- **Contracts**: Always read the fine print or have someone you trust explain it to you

Rule of Thumb: **"If it sounds too good, it's probably too shady."**

11. Financial Mindset for Student-Athlete Entrepreneurs

- **Treat NIL Like a Business**:
- Track income and expenses
- Set aside money for taxes
- Keep personal and brand spending separate
- **Start Simple**:
- Budget, save, and plan for both today and tomorrow
- Don't fall into the trap of lifestyle creep ("look rich" vs. **be rich**)

Takeaway: Just like you train your body, you've got to train your financial habits and your business mindset.

12. Personal Mission & Brand Purpose

- What do you want to be known for **beyond the game**?
- What impact do you want to have in your community, your country, or your sport?
- Align your NIL work with your core values—brands notice, and followers respect it.

Think about:

> *"If someone Googled me five years from now, what would I want them to see?"*

Final Thought for Section V:

You don't need a million followers or a national TV deal to build a brand that lasts.

All you need is your story, your values, and a little bit of vision.

This section is your blueprint—not just to monetize your name, but to build something **that represents who you are and where you're going.**

Chapter 17: NIL for Women in International Sports

"You are the brand, the business, and the blueprint for what's possible."

For many international female athletes, NIL is not just a new income stream—it's a game-changing opportunity to turn talent, story, and voice into influence and income. And while male-dominated sports like football and basketball often grab headlines, many of the most creative, successful NIL earners are women—especially international women in sports like gymnastics, volleyball, tennis, and track & field.

This chapter is all about helping you—as a female international athlete—understand your value, build your platform with confidence, and make the most of your NIL opportunities, all while staying safe, strategic, and true to who you are.

Unique NIL Opportunities for Women in Sport

Social media has leveled the playing field in many ways. Female athletes—especially those in sports with visual storytelling potential like gymnastics, volleyball, and tennis—have massive opportunities for:

- Brand partnerships and product ambassadorships
- Content creation (training tips, lifestyle, recovery, beauty, health)

- Public speaking or motivational platforms
- Academic or cultural ambassador roles
- Long-term entrepreneurship and mentorship

Many brands are drawn to the authenticity, engagement, and storytelling that female athletes bring. NIL research shows that 68% of top female NIL earners come from women's sports, especially those with strong social or visual presence.

Creative Niches That Work:

- Behind-the-scenes training content
- Academic-focused branding (study hacks, student-athlete life)
- Mental health and body image advocacy
- Health and wellness content (smoothie recipes, stretching routines)
- Bilingual content that bridges U.S. and international audiences

Don't be afraid to own your lane. Your unique background is your advantage.

Navigating Gender Biases and Staying Safe

Unfortunately, being a woman in sports—and on social media—comes with added risks. While opportunities are expanding, so are expectations and, sometimes, dangerous assumptions.

Common Challenges:

- Objectification or inappropriate DMs
- Pressure to look or behave a certain way to attract sponsorships
- Assumptions that your value is only in appearance, not performance
- Safety risks associated with increased visibility and personal sharing

Safety Tips:

- **Never share your real-time location**
- **Keep personal details off public posts** (phone number, address, daily schedule)
- **Use business email accounts** for NIL deals and limit personal DMs
- **Review all contracts** with a trusted adult, mentor, or legal professional
- **Consider a private vs. public account strategy**

You can be visible without being vulnerable. Set the terms for your presence.

Case Studies: Female Athletes Winning With NIL

Gymnast from South America

This athlete started small, posting bilingual captions that connected her with fans in both the U.S. and her home country. Her behind-the-scenes content showing recovery, mindset, and technique gained traction. She attracted fitness brands and grew a YouTube following focused on tutorials.

Volleyball Player from Eastern Europe

She built a following by staying true to her values—emphasizing body confidence, strength, and education. She landed NIL deals with a skincare company and a nutrition brand, proving that personal alignment is as powerful as metrics.

Tennis Player from Asia

Using NIL earnings, she launched her own branded tennis apparel. She collaborated with mental health campaigns and developed a platform around self-discipline and empowerment, becoming a role model in her home country.

These athletes didn't wait for permission. They used NIL to tell their story on their terms.

Tips for Negotiating NIL Deals With Confidence

You're not just a student-athlete—you're a businesswoman. And you deserve to approach NIL deals with knowledge and assertiveness.

Know Your Value:

- Brands want authenticity, not just follower count
- You bring global reach, multilingual access, and community credibility
- Track your analytics (engagement rate, audience demographics, reach)

Ask Smart Questions:

- What do you expect from me in this partnership?
- How long is the agreement?
- What rights do you want to my content or image?
- Can I approve all messaging before it goes live?
- What's the compensation structure (flat fee, affiliate, commission)?

Watch Out For Red Flags:

- Vague contracts or verbal-only agreements
- Unclear expectations or deliverables
- Brands that pressure you to change your image or values
- Anyone who says, "This is exposure, not payment"

Always read contracts. And don't be afraid to walk away.

Using Your Platform for Advocacy and Empowerment

You don't have to go pro to go big. Your story, voice, and platform can be powerful tools for change.

Ways to Lead with Purpose:

- Advocate for **mental health** in women's sports
- Use your voice for **body positivity** and self-worth
- Share nutrition and recovery tips for young athletes
- Highlight cultural traditions or holidays
- Fundraise for causes in your home country

Use NIL to create community, not just cash.

Building a Strong Online Presence

You don't have to be an influencer. You just need to be intentional.

Social Media Tips:

- Use dual-language captions
- Post a mix of training, personality, and behind-the-scenes
- Be consistent, not perfect
- Use stories and polls

Chapter 18: NIL and Mental Health – Protecting Your Mind While Building Your Brand

"You are your greatest asset. Protect your mind the way you protect your name."

Being a student-athlete is hard. Being an international student-athlete trying to balance college, sports, and a public brand is even harder. As NIL opportunities continue to grow, so do the pressures. For many international athletes, what was once a dream—competing in the U.S., building a platform, supporting family back home—can quickly become overwhelming.

This chapter dives deep into the emotional, psychological, and practical realities of managing your mental health while navigating the fast-paced world of NIL. We explore stress, burnout, boundaries, cultural barriers, and tools for maintaining well-being as your platform grows.

The Emotional Weight of Being Far from Home

Imagine being thousands of miles away from your support system—family, childhood friends, your native language, and everything familiar. Now add in the stress of performance, the responsibility of a scholarship, and the added visibility of NIL deals.

International student-athletes carry emotional pressure that many others may never fully understand:

- Feeling like you have to "make it" to justify leaving home
- Carrying guilt for not being physically there to support family
- Feeling isolated due to language or cultural differences
- Navigating time zone challenges just to stay in touch
- Adjusting to a new academic and social culture

All of this can take a toll on your mental well-being. Add NIL expectations on top, and the emotional bandwidth required becomes even greater.

When NIL Becomes Pressure Instead of Power

NIL opportunities can be exciting, empowering, and life-changing. But if you're not careful, they can also lead to:

- **Burnout** from trying to manage content creation, events, classes, and training
- **Anxiety** over sponsorship deliverables, contract details, and perfor mance
- **Imposter syndrome** if you feel unqualified to represent a brand
- **Comparison fatigue** from constantly measuring your success against others
- **Public scrutiny** that creates pressure to "always be on"

It's important to ask yourself: "Am I still in control of my NIL journey, or is it starting to control me?"

Setting Boundaries to Protect Your Peace

Your time, energy, and attention are limited. Boundaries are how you protect them.

Boundaries with Social Media:

- Set screen time limits using your phone settings.
- Unfollow accounts that trigger comparison or anxiety.
- Schedule time **off** social media weekly.
- Remember that social media is a highlight reel—not reality.

Boundaries with NIL Commitments:

- Create “NIL hours” in your week to work on brand-related tasks.
- Don’t accept every deal. Ask: “Does this align with my goals and values?”
- Be clear with agents or managers about your availability.

Boundaries with Friends and Family:

- Communicate when you’re overwhelmed.
- Be honest about financial or emotional pressures.
- Ask for emotional support—not just encouragement to keep grinding.

Setting boundaries isn’t selfish. It’s **necessary** for your survival and success.

Where to Find Mental Health Support on Campus

Many colleges offer free or low-cost mental health resources for students. Here are a few to explore:

Campus Counseling Centers:

- Offer one-on-one therapy sessions (often covered by tuition)
- May provide group therapy for student-athletes
- Often have culturally competent counselors

International Student Services:

- Help with visa-related stress or cultural adjustment
- Provide guidance on healthcare access and insurance

Athletic Department Mental Health Coordinators:

- Specific resources for athletes
- Often available without a referral

Peer Support Groups:

- Connect with other international students or athletes
- Safe space to talk about stress, burnout, and identity

Online Therapy Apps (Check with your school for free access):

- Headspace, Calm, BetterHelp, Talkspace

You're not weak for asking for help. You're **wise** for knowing when to reach out.

Self-Care That Actually Works

Self-care isn't all spa days and scented candles. Sometimes, it's discipline. Other times, it's doing less.

Physical Self-Care:

- Hydrate (water is your best performance booster)
- Sleep 7–9 hours consistently
- Move your body outside of training—walks, yoga, or stretching

Emotional Self-Care:

- Journal your thoughts
- Talk to someone you trust
- Take breaks from digital noise

Mental Self-Care:

- Prioritize rest over hustle
- Say "no" when you're at capacity
- Plan your week to reduce decision fatigue

Rule of Thumb: You can't pour from an empty cup. Fill yours first.

Support Systems: Build One, Use One

You need more than ambition—you need people. Build a team off the field:

- **Teammates:** The only ones who understand your daily grind
- **Coaches:** Can help adjust expectations if you're struggling
- **Professors:** May offer flexibility if you're overwhelmed
- **Family:** Stay connected, even if it's a 10-minute call
- **Mentors:** NIL advisors, brand reps, or older athletes

Your network is your safety net. Lean on them.

Planning NIL Around Your Mental Health

NIL shouldn't be an afterthought—but it also shouldn't consume you.

Try This Weekly Planner:

TimeFocus

Morning

Training + Class

Midday

Rest + Food + Study

Late Afternoon

NIL tasks (1–2 hours)

Evening

Homework + Downtime

Night

Relax + Unplug

Flexibility is key. Don't punish yourself for not doing everything. Adjust weekly based on your physical and emotional energy.

Know the Signs: When to Get Help

Watch for these mental health red flags:

- Difficulty sleeping or oversleeping
- Changes in appetite or energy
- Feeling disconnected from friends or teammates
- Losing interest in things you love
- Trouble concentrating or remembering
- Feeling hopeless, anxious, or irritable for long periods

If you check multiple boxes, don't try to "tough it out."

Talk to someone.

What Coaches and Teammates Should Know

If you're reading this as a coach, teammate, or mentor—here's how you can support athletes in the NIL space:

- Normalize mental health check-ins
- Praise rest, not just hustle
- Model boundaries and balance
- Encourage therapy as part of training
- Watch for warning signs of burnout

We rise together, or not at all.

Final Word: You're Not Alone, and You're Not a Brand

You are a full person—not just a performer, a student, or an influencer. Yes, NIL can open doors. But mental health **keeps you strong enough** to walk through them.

You don't owe anyone constant content. You don't have to do it all. And you absolutely do not have to suffer in silence.

Take care of your mind. Take care of your heart. And trust that the most valuable thing you can ever protect—is you.

Chapter 19: Managing Peer Pressure and Lifestyle Inflation

"Just because you can spend it doesn't mean you should."

In the NIL era, the pressure to "look the part" has never been stronger. You might find yourself comparing your lifestyle, gear, or social media presence to that of teammates, influencers, or pro athletes. It's easy to feel like you need to spend money to prove success—especially when the spotlight is on. But remember: NIL is not just about making money. It's about managing it wisely, aligning it with your values, and planning for your future.

This chapter explores how to recognize and resist peer pressure and lifestyle inflation, how to protect your long-term financial goals, and why the athletes who live modestly often come out ahead.

The Pressure to Look Successful

When teammates post new cars, designer clothes, or luxury trips, it can create an invisible pressure to "keep up."

Common Pressures:

- Feeling the need to upgrade your wardrobe or accessories
- Buying expensive items to "celebrate" NIL deals
- Attending every party, trip, or event to stay relevant
- Accepting deals for products or appearances you don't believe in

Ask Yourself:

- Am I doing this because I want to—or because others are?
- Is this helping me grow, or is it just for show?

Short-Term Flash vs. Long-Term Wealth

NIL money can come fast—but it can also disappear just as quickly. The athletes who win the financial game are not always the loudest or most visible. They're the ones who make smart, consistent choices behind the scenes.

Flash:

- Designer brands
- Expensive meals
- Frequent travel
- One-time deals for instant cash

Wealth:

- Emergency savings
- Investing in index funds or IRAs
- Paying off debt
- Building a brand you control

Remember: Flexing fades. Freedom lasts.

Saying No with Confidence

Saying no is a skill—and a superpower. It helps you:

- Avoid deals that don't align with your values
- Save time, money, and energy
- Focus on your personal and professional goals

How to Say No:

- "Thank you, but that doesn't fit with my brand."
- "I'm focusing on long-term partnerships right now."
- "I'm going to pass, but I appreciate the offer."

Whether it's a NIL deal, a night out, or a group purchase, know that saying no is not weakness—it's wisdom.

Staying Grounded in High-Visibility Spaces

NIL visibility can change how people treat you. More attention can mean more opportunities—but also more pressure.

Stay Grounded By:

- Surrounding yourself with people who support your true self
- Reflecting regularly on your goals and values
- Giving back or mentoring others
- Remembering where you came from and why you started

You don't have to prove anything to anyone. Your path is yours to walk.

The Quiet Earners Win the Long Game

You won't always see the athletes who are saving, investing, and planning. They're not posting every dollar. But they're building quietly, confidently, and with intention.

They're:

- Buying their first property before age 25
- Graduating debt-free
- Launching businesses or foundations
- Setting up their families for generational wealth

Let your legacy be more than what you wore or where you went. Let it be what you built.

Final Word: Choose Your Own Pace

In a world that rewards appearance, choose substance. In a game that moves fast, choose patience. In a system that pressures you to spend, choose purpose.

Peer pressure is real. But so is personal power.

Stay smart. Stay grounded. And remember: Quiet money moves loud in the future.

Chapter 20: How to Vet Professionals—Agents, Advisors, and Influencers

"Trust is earned, not assumed."

As an athlete navigating NIL, you will encounter people offering help. Some will be legitimate experts who want to guide your success. Others will be looking to take advantage of your inexperience, your earnings, or your name. Whether it's an agent in your DMs, a financial advisor promising big returns, or an influencer pitching a quick collab, your ability to vet professionals can protect your brand, your money, and your peace of mind.

This chapter teaches you how to separate value from vultures—and how to build a trustworthy team around your NIL journey.

Do Your Homework Before Saying Yes

Before signing anything, agreeing to a call, or giving access to your personal info, take the time to research the person or company contacting you.

Steps to Vet a Professional:

- Google their name + company
- Look at their LinkedIn profile for experience and education
- Check for news articles, reviews, or complaints
- Ask who else they work with
- Search for their name in combination with the word "scam"

Don't rush into a partnership because it "feels right." Do your due diligence first.

Red Flags to Watch Out For

Some warning signs that should make you slow down or walk away:

In DMs:

- They promise to "make you a millionaire fast"
- Their profile is vague or recently created
- They have no official business website or public presence

In Contracts:

- There's no end date (meaning it lasts forever)
- There's a high percentage commission or vague payment terms
- You don't understand the language and they pressure you to sign anyway

In Behavior:

- They refuse to explain how they get paid
- They discourage you from getting a second opinion
- They badmouth your school, coach, or family

Questions to Ask Before Signing

Don't be afraid to interview professionals the same way they're evaluating you. You have every right to ask questions.

Ask:

- What is your background and who else have you worked with?
- How do you get paid? Is it commission, flat fee, or something else?
- Can I talk to another athlete or client you've helped?
- Will you involve my coach, family, or compliance officer in this process?
- Can I have a copy of the contract to review for 48 hours?

Checking for Credentials

Some professionals need licenses or certifications to legally give advice.

Agents:

- Must be registered with your state or league (ask for proof)
- Should follow NCAA or school-specific NIL regulations

Financial Advisors:

- Check if they are a CFP (Certified Financial Planner) or registered with the SEC/FINRA
- Search their name at www.brokercheck.finra.org

Lawyers:

- Should be licensed in their state (check with state bar website)
- Should specialize in contracts or sports/entertainment law

Don't let fancy titles or social media followers fool you. Credentials matter.

Get a Second Opinion

Even if someone checks all the boxes, you should still get a second opinion:

- Ask your school's compliance officer to review the deal
- Run the opportunity by a trusted professor, coach, or mentor
- Talk to other athletes who've worked with them

Taking 48 hours to review a decision is smart. Being rushed into something usually means **they** benefit more than **you**.

Keep Your School in the Loop

Your school's compliance team is there to protect your eligibility and keep you informed.

What They Can Do:

- Review contracts for red flags
- Ensure the deal doesn't violate school or NCAA rules
- Help you avoid tax or visa issues (especially for international students)
- Guide you toward reputable professionals they trust

Looping in your school doesn't make you look weak—it shows maturity and professionalism.

Final Word: Choose Wisely, Stay in Control

You are the CEO of your NIL journey. That means you get to decide who joins your team. Choose people who:

- Respect your goals
- Explain things clearly
- Have a track record of honesty and service
- Want to educate and empower you, not just profit off you

Trust is earned. Keep your standards high, your questions ready, and your future protected.

Chapter 21: NIL and Taxes in Your Home Country

"Earning globally means planning locally—and legally."

As an international student-athlete earning money through Name, Image, and Likeness (NIL), it's important to understand that your financial obligations don't end at the U.S. border. While the IRS (Internal Revenue Service) in the United States expects you to report and pay taxes on your NIL income, your home country might also have expectations.

Failing to plan for taxes in both countries can result in confusion, penalties, or even long-term legal trouble. This chapter will walk you through what you need to know about taxes in your home country, how to prepare for cross-border financial issues, and how to protect your earnings and your future.

What Your Home Country Might Expect You to Report

Each country has its own tax laws. Some tax you only on income earned within the country. Others tax citizens and residents on **worldwide income**. That means if you're a citizen or resident of a country with global taxation rules, you may be required to report your NIL earnings to **your home tax authority**.

Common Home-Country Tax Expectations:

- Report all income earned abroad (including NIL money, endorsements, brand deals)
- Convert income from U.S. dollars to local currency
- File an annual tax return, even while living abroad
- Disclose foreign bank accounts and business interests

Questions to Ask Yourself:

- Does my country tax foreign income?
- Do I have to declare NIL money even if it was earned in the U.S.?
- Will this income affect family benefits, tuition assistance, or government support?

Dual Taxation and Currency Conversion

The fear of "being taxed twice" is a real concern for many international earners. Fortunately, many countries have **tax treaties** with the United States to avoid this.

Key Concepts:

- **Foreign Tax Credit**: If you pay taxes in the U.S., your home country may give you credit so you aren't double-taxed.
- **Currency Conversion**: You'll need to convert your NIL income into local currency using official exchange rates, usually based on when you received the income.
- **Tax Residency Rules**: Spending too much time in either country might trigger tax residency, which could change your filing requirements.

Ask a professional how these apply to your specific country.

Work With a Cross-Border Tax Advisor

NIL income, like any international income, requires **specialized help**. Your regular accountant or family member might not understand the unique challenges of earning abroad.

What a Cross-Border Tax Advisor Can Help You With:

- Determining whether you owe taxes in your home country
- Filing in both countries properly
- Understanding tax treaties and double taxation rules
- Handling remittances or wire transfers safely

Look for advisors who:

- Work with international students or athletes
- Understand U.S. and home country tax law
- Can communicate in your language, if needed

Keep Detailed Records

Whether or not you owe taxes back home, **you need to keep good records**. This protects you from audits, errors, and surprises.

Track:

- How much you earned (every NIL payment, product, or freebie has value)
- When you received it (date of transaction)
- How it was paid (bank, app, cash, etc.)
- Who paid you (brand, agency, etc.)
- Exchange rates on the day of each payment

Create a folder with copies of:

- Invoices
- Contracts
- 1099 or W-8BEN forms
- Emails about payments or partnerships
- Tax returns (U.S. and home country)

How NIL Might Affect Your Family or Benefits Back Home

In some countries, if you earn money abroad, it could impact:

- Your family's eligibility for benefits
- Tuition subsidies or public health insurance
- Your own tax status or government scholarship support
- Inheritance or asset reporting laws

Be transparent with your family and advisors back home. If needed, consult a local accountant or legal expert who understands how foreign income is treated in your country.

Final Word: Don't Let Confusion Cost You

You worked hard for your NIL income. Don't risk losing it to poor planning or a missed tax filing. Taxes can be complicated, but they can also be managed with the right tools and support.

Remember:

- You are responsible for following both U.S. and home country laws
- Start planning early, not just when filing season begins
- The right professionals can save you more than they cost
- Keep your paperwork organized and ask for help when you need it

Your NIL success is international. Your tax planning should be too.

Chapter 22: Creating a Legacy with NIL – Giving Back and Building for Others

"A legacy isn't just what you leave behind. It's what you build while you're here."

Earning from your name, image, and likeness is an incredible opportunity—but what you do with it beyond the bank account is what truly defines your impact. As an international student-athlete, your story already bridges cultures, challenges norms, and opens doors. Now imagine what happens when you use that platform to lift others.

This chapter explores how NIL can become a force for good—whether it's in your home country, your school community, or a cause you believe in. Giving back doesn't always mean giving money. It can mean offering time, mentorship, representation, or inspiration. But like all things in financial planning, it works best when it's done with purpose.

Using Your NIL Platform to Make a Difference

Social media influence, visibility, and sponsorships are powerful tools. And while many athletes focus only on personal branding or profits, others are discovering how to use their NIL voice to lead, serve, and change lives.

Ways to Use Your Platform:

- Raise awareness for global or local issues
- Spotlight underfunded programs at home or school
- Create content focused on education, health, or youth development
- Amplify voices in your community that don't get national attention
- Share your personal journey as motivation

Giving Back to Your Home Country or Local Community

Your success can ripple outward—especially when shared intentionally. Many international athletes find joy and purpose in reinvesting their time, money, or story back home.

Ideas for Giving Back:

- Start or support a youth sports program in your hometown
- Partner with a nonprofit doing work in your country
- Donate equipment, uniforms, or school supplies
- Host virtual workshops or Q&As for young athletes
- Provide translation or cultural support at your school or team

Remember, it's not about how much you give. It's about showing that you care and being consistent.

Scholarships, Mentorships, and Partnerships

One of the most powerful things you can do is help create access for someone else.

Ways to Build Access:

- Create a scholarship fund at your school, church, or sports club
- Offer one-on-one or group mentoring for young athletes
- Collaborate with brands or donors to support youth clinics

- Work with faculty to support international student initiatives
- Join or build ambassador programs focused on equity and diversity

You don't have to wait until you're a millionaire. You just need a mission.

Balancing Generosity with Financial Responsibility

Giving is noble. But it's not an excuse to ignore your own needs. Don't feel pressured to give beyond your means. Make generosity a **part** of your plan, not your entire plan.

Smart Giving Tips:

- Set a monthly or annual giving budget
- Use part of NIL earnings to support causes—while still saving and investing
- Talk with a financial advisor or trusted mentor about your giving goals
- Be transparent with family or organizations about what you can (and can't) do

Rule of Thumb: Give from overflow, not obligation. You'll be more joyful and consistent.

Creating Long-Term Impact with Values-Based Planning

Legacy isn't about how much you earn. It's about what your life says when you're no longer in the room.

Steps to Build Values-Based Legacy:

1. Define what matters to you most (education, equity, faith, opportunity?)
2. Align your NIL choices with those values
3. Build your brand around purpose, not just popularity

4. Set short- and long-term giving goals
5. Include giving in your financial planning (tax write-offs, charitable accounts, etc.)

You might not change the world overnight. But you can change one life today—and build a foundation to change more tomorrow.

Final Word: You Are the Legacy

Every follower, every partnership, every dollar earned through NIL is a chance to say something meaningful.

You don't need a foundation to have purpose. You don't need a million followers to lead. You just need intention, action, and heart.

Build for yourself. Build for your family. But also, build for others.

Because your name, image, and likeness are powerful. But your impact? That's your true legacy.

Chapter 23: Banking and Investing — How to Open the Right Accounts

As an international student-athlete in the U.S., your money journey starts with something simple but powerful: **opening the right accounts.** Whether you're getting your first NIL deal or working a part-time job, you'll need a safe and legal place to deposit money, pay bills, and—eventually—**invest for your future**.

In this chapter, we'll walk you through:

- How to open a U.S. **bank account**
- How to open an **investment account**
- What documents you'll need
- The difference between **Roth IRAs**, **Traditional IRAs**, and **Taxable Accounts**
- Common mistakes to avoid
- How to stay compliant as an international student

Let's get started.

Step 1: Open a U.S. Bank Account

You'll need a checking and possibly a savings account to receive payments, shop online, pay rent, and manage everyday expenses. Most NIL income will go directly into your bank account via direct deposit, Venmo, Zelle, or

PayPal—which all require a U.S. account.

What You Need to Open a Bank Account (as an international student):
Most banks will ask for:

1. **Passport**
2. **Student Visa (F-1 or J-1)**
3. **I-20 Form (Certificate of Eligibility)**
4. **Proof of U.S. Address** (a utility bill, dorm lease, or letter from your school)
5. **School ID or acceptance letter**
6. **Social Security Number (SSN)** or **Individual Taxpayer Identification Number (ITIN)** — *some banks allow you to open an account without one, but many will require it to use full features or earn interest.*

Tip: *Choose a bank with a local branch near your school and low or no monthly maintenance fees for students.*

Types of Accounts to Open:

- **Checking Account** (for daily spending, NIL income, bills)
- **Savings Account** (for short-term goals or emergency funds)

Step 2: Understand Your Rights and Responsibilities

Once you open an account:

- Monitor it regularly using your bank's mobile app
- Don't let others deposit or withdraw money for you—**you are responsible for all activity**
- Be mindful of overdraft fees
- Avoid using your account for non-NIL business if your visa restricts work

> ***Important:*** *You can't legally earn income* outside *your visa terms. Any income that violates F-1 rules could put your immigration status at risk. That's why it's critical to only accept deals that have been approved by your school's compliance office.*

Step 3: Opening an Investment Account in the U.S.

Once you've saved a few thousand dollars and covered your immediate expenses, **it's time to think long-term.** Investing can help you grow your NIL money, especially if you don't need to spend it right away.

But not all investment accounts are right—or even *available*—for international students.

Types of Accounts to Consider:

1. Taxable Investment Account

- **Most flexible option** for international students
- No income or contribution limits
- Can buy stocks, ETFs, mutual funds, etc.
- **You'll owe taxes on gains** (capital gains, dividends)

> Best option if you don't have a U.S. Social Security Number or if your visa status doesn't allow retirement contributions

2. Roth IRA *(Retirement Account)*

- Funded with after-tax money
- Grows tax-free and withdrawals are tax-free in retirement
- 2025 contribution limit: $7,000 (if under age 50)
- **Only available if you have U.S.-taxable earned income and a Social Security Number**

> If your NIL money is considered self-employment income and you file taxes properly, you may qualify. But check with a tax advisor

or CPA to be sure.

3. Traditional IRA

- Similar to Roth, but contributions may be tax-deductible (depending on your income)
- Taxed when withdrawn in retirement

Key Difference: *Roth = pay taxes now, none later. Traditional = no taxes now, pay later.*

What You Need to Open an Investment Account

Whether it's with a brokerage firm (like Fidelity, Schwab, Vanguard, or a digital platform like Robinhood or M1 Finance), you'll typically need:

- **Name and Date of Birth**
- **Valid Passport and Visa**
- **SSN or ITIN** *(some brokerages allow ITIN only)*
- **U.S. Address**
- **U.S. Bank Account (for funding the account)**
- **Tax residency declaration** (W-8BEN form for nonresident aliens)

Best Practices for First-Time Investors

1. **Start small.** \$50–\$100 per month is a great start. Let your money grow with time.
2. **Stick to diversified ETFs** (like S&P 500 funds) if you're unsure where to begin.
3. **Avoid day trading or crypto hype** unless you fully understand the risks.
4. **Don't invest money you need in the short term.**
5. **Keep track of your tax documents.** You'll receive a 1099-B or 1042-S

each year.

Warning: *Some brokerages may not allow international students to open accounts without a SSN. Call their customer service first and ask about international or non-resident alien options.*

Common Mistakes to Avoid

- **Using a friend's U.S. address or SSN to open accounts** – this is illegal and can jeopardize your visa
- **Assuming all income can be invested** – *make sure it's legal income based on your visa*
- **Overlooking tax reporting** – investment income, even small, must be reported
- **Not asking for help** – international students often miss opportunities simply because they're afraid to ask

Final Thoughts: Start Where You Are

You don't need to be rich to open an account. You just need to be ready.

Your NIL money shouldn't sit under your mattress or vanish on impulse spending. Set up the right accounts. Learn how they work. Ask smart questions. And start building wealth today—with *intention.*

Because even if your stay in the U.S. is temporary, your financial habits will follow you for life.

Chapter 24: NIL Stories From International Athletes

Sometimes the best way to learn is through someone else's story.

Not theory. Not guidelines.

But *real-life choices, challenges, and lessons.*

In this chapter, we'll spotlight the journeys of several international student-athletes navigating NIL in different ways. These are **fictionalized** composites—based on true events, interviews, and common scenarios that international athletes face every season.

The names are changed, but the situations are real.

Story 1: Amara from Nigeria – "The Tax Bill I Didn't See Coming"

Amara was a standout sprinter from Lagos competing at a Division I university in Texas. After her sophomore season, a track apparel brand offered her $4,500 to do a few sponsored Instagram posts. She was thrilled—finally, she could help pay for flights to visit her family and send money back home.

But she didn't realize the $4,500 was considered **self-employment income**, and that **no taxes were withheld** from the payment. No one explained to her that as a 1099 contractor, she'd owe **federal and possibly state income tax**—even on just a few thousand dollars.

The next spring, she got a surprise: a tax bill from the IRS—and she didn't have the money saved.

Lesson: Even small NIL payments count as income. Always set aside 20–30% for taxes. Ask your school's compliance office or an international tax advisor for help before you accept money.

Story 2: Leif from Sweden – "The Brand That Wanted Too Much"

Leif, a basketball player from Stockholm, was contacted by a fitness company on social media. They loved his highlight clips and offered him a deal: post twice a week and appear in one livestream workout for $200/month.

What Leif didn't notice was the fine print in the contract that gave the company **lifetime rights** to use his name, image, and video clips—even *after* the partnership ended.

When Leif transferred to another school and started building his own brand, he saw his old workout videos still being promoted by the company—without his permission. They refused to take the content down because, technically, they didn't have to.

Lesson: Read every contract carefully. Watch out for *perpetual usage rights, exclusivity,* and vague language. When in doubt, bring in a school legal advisor or outside expert before signing.

Story 3: Hana from Japan – "Cultural Pressure and Saying 'No'"

Hana was a tennis player from Tokyo with a growing social media presence. She was offered an NIL deal from a local apparel brand, but her parents back home were hesitant. They believed it might distract her from school, and culturally, they felt that asking for money or promoting herself too much was not respectful.

Hana didn't want to disappoint them, so she turned the deal down—even though it was small and manageable. Months later, she saw teammates building their brands and realized she could have accepted the offer *on her terms*—with boundaries and balance.

She eventually worked with her parents to set clear limits: only one campaign per semester, and she had to stay on top of school. With trust and communication, she landed a new opportunity that honored both her goals *and* her family values.

Lesson: Every athlete's path is unique. Cultural expectations matter. But with open conversation and boundaries, NIL can be done in a way that respects your background while growing your future.

Story 4: Mateo from Argentina – "Making NIL Work Without Breaking Visa Rules"

Mateo, a soccer player on an F-1 visa, learned the hard way that he couldn't accept *cash-based NIL deals* without risking his visa. He was offered $1,000 by a local soccer training academy to do a weekend clinic—but technically, it was considered off-campus work and not allowed under F-1 guidelines.

Luckily, Mateo double-checked with his school's international office before saying yes. They confirmed that accepting that deal could violate his visa and potentially put his student status at risk.

Instead, they helped him identify a brand partnership that *paid him through a U.S. collective structure,* which was properly documented and did not conflict with visa guidelines. Mateo got paid—and kept his legal status safe.

Lesson: If you're an international student-athlete, always check with both the **school compliance office** *and* the **international student office** before accepting any deal. Even small payments could lead to immigration issues.

Story 5: Lita from Tonga – "The Power of Her Story"

Lita, a rugby player from Tonga playing at a U.S. university on the West Coast, didn't think NIL was "for someone like her." She wasn't a top scorer, she didn't have a huge social media following, and English was her second language.

But one day, she told her story—how she started playing barefoot in the islands, how her community fundraised to send her overseas, and what it meant to represent her country. The video was picked up by her school's media team and went viral.

Within a few weeks, she had brand offers—not because of stats, but because of **authenticity**. She partnered with a nonprofit that supports Pacific Islander athletes, and now she's using NIL to give back to girls in her hometown.

Lesson: NIL isn't just about fame—it's about story, identity, and purpose. Your voice matters, even if your follower count is small.

Final Thoughts: Learn From Their Journey—Shape Your Own

These stories show the wide range of experiences international athletes face in the NIL world. Some are about wins. Some are about regrets. But they all carry lessons you can apply right now.

- Read contracts.
- Ask questions.
- Honor your culture.
- Know your legal limits.
- Protect your money.
- Use your story with pride.

You're not alone in this. And you don't have to figure it all out by yourself. Learn from the paths of others, build your own roadmap, and keep moving forward—smartly, boldly, and on your terms.

SECTION VI: SPORTS-SPECIFIC STRATEGIES

Not all sports are treated equally when it comes to NIL.

Each has its own **audience, brand potential, and content style**—and as an international athlete, your approach should reflect your **sport's culture** and your **personal voice**.

Here's how to **leverage your sport** the smart way:

Basketball

- **High NIL ceiling**—especially for elite programs and televised games
- Strong culture around **highlight reels, sneakers, and fashion**
- Players often go viral on social media due to skill, flash, and charisma

Tips:

- Control your image—what you post matters
- Share training routines, game-day fits, sneaker reviews
- Collaborate with photographers and content creators to stand out visually

Football

- Male-dominated NIL space with **high deal values**—but not for every player
- **Quarterbacks and skill positions** get the most attention, but linemen can win with humor, motivation, or niche appeal

Tips:

- Focus on **team culture**, strength videos, and leadership off the field
- Use **Twitter and Instagram Reels** to show personality
- Create value by being authentic—even if you don't touch the ball every play

Soccer

- Global sport = **global audience potential**
- Leverage your **multilingual skills and cultural identity** for branding

Tips:

- Post game footage with commentary in English + your native language
- Share recovery, nutrition, or travel stories that resonate with fans worldwide
- Male athletes can focus on drills/highlights; female athletes often thrive with lifestyle + BTS content

Volleyball

- **Exploding NIL space for women**, especially in D-I programs
- Content thrives on **Instagram, TikTok**, and YouTube Shorts

Tips:

- Share **day-in-the-life, pre-game rituals, and training tips**
- Use **bright, positive visuals** and relatable captions
- Lean into teaching: jump tutorials, setting tips, workouts

Tennis

- International by nature—your **audience already spans continents**
- NIL potential through **individual sponsorships, gear deals, and content monetization**

Tips:

- Offer short-form **coaching tips, match breakdowns, or Q&As**
- Review racquets, grips, training tools, or court gear
- Explore NIL during breaks **while abroad** to avoid visa issues

Track & Field

- Focused fanbase = **loyal niche following**
- Performance highlights are the core of your brand
- NIL success often comes through **fitness and wellness partnerships**

Tips:

- Post race-day routines, running form tips, and competition vlogs
- Partner with hydration brands, running shoe companies, or supplement lines
- Use Instagram for photo storytelling, YouTube for long-form race content

SECTION VII: BUILDING LONG-TERM WEALTH

It's not just about **making** money—it's about **keeping** it, growing it, and using it wisely.

Here's how to take your NIL, stipend, or savings and **build a financial foundation that lasts far beyond sports.**

11. Saving, Investing & Sending Money Home

Money moves fast—unless you tell it where to go.

Start with the basics, then scale your strategy as your income and understanding grow.

Emergency Fund

- Save **3–6 months** of living expenses (rent, food, travel)
- Keep it in a separate **savings account**, not your checking

Why it matters: This gives you **breathing room** if unexpected expenses hit—like travel, injuries, or delays in payments.

Opening U.S. Bank Accounts

- Choose a **student-friendly bank** (low or no fees)
- Use one **checking account** for daily spending
- Use one **savings account** for long-term and emergency money

Pro Tip: Set up **automatic transfers** from checking to savings monthly.

Basics of Investing

Even small amounts grow over time—start early.

- Learn about **index funds** (like S&P 500 ETFs)
- If you become eligible (via OPT or earned income), open a **Roth IRA**
- Avoid high-risk "get rich quick" schemes—stick to basics

Rule of Thumb: If you **don't understand it, don't invest in it.**

Sending Money Home Safely

- Use reliable platforms like **Wise, Remitly, or Xoom**
- Watch out for **exchange rate fees** and **hidden transfer costs**
- Keep records of large transfers for **tax purposes**

Tip: Don't carry large cash amounts—keep it digital and secure.

12. Giving Back and Staying Grounded

You've made it far—and you didn't do it alone.

Whether it's family, coaches, community, or culture—**giving back keeps you connected to your "why."**

Philanthropy While Abroad

- Share your story to raise awareness
- Organize fundraisers or donation drives for causes back home
- Use your NIL platform to highlight real issues—not just products

Highlighting Causes From Your Home Country

Whether it's:

- Access to clean water
- Youth sports development
- Mental health awareness
- Education for girls
- Use your platform for **something bigger than yourself**.

Partnerships With Purpose

Look for brands that:

- Support causes you believe in
- Let you lead with authenticity
- Align with your identity, values, or culture

You're not just an athlete—you're a role model.

Rule of Thumb:

> ***"Giving back pays forward."***

It keeps you grounded.
It builds real influence.
And it reminds you: this isn't just about money—it's about meaning.

Chapter 25: Planning for Professional Sports (Domestic & International)

You've trained for years. You've competed at the college level. You've built a name, maybe even landed some NIL deals. Now, the next big question is: **Can you make this your career?**

For many student-athletes—especially international ones—the dream is to go pro. Whether that's in the U.S., your home country, or elsewhere around the world, the path forward is exciting but also filled with financial, legal, and logistical challenges.

This chapter is here to help you make a **realistic, strategic game plan**—so you're not just chasing a dream, you're *building a career.*

The Dream vs. The Details

It's easy to get caught up in the vision: pro stadiums, sponsorships, international travel, getting paid to play the sport you love. But the truth is, **only a small percentage of college athletes go pro**—and of those who do, not all earn big contracts or long-term deals.

That doesn't mean you can't do it. It just means: **you need a plan, not just a hope.**

Step 1: Define What "Pro" Means to You

Professional sports don't just exist in the NBA, NFL, MLB, or top European soccer leagues. Going pro could mean:

- Playing in a smaller international league
- Competing in a domestic pro tour (e.g., tennis, track, rugby, volleyball)
- Signing with a development or minor league
- Turning your athletic skills into coaching, training, or media work
- Launching a business or digital brand that builds on your sport

Knowing your end goal helps you reverse-engineer the steps you'll need to get there.

Step 2: Understand Eligibility, Timing, and Visas

If you're planning to go pro in the **United States**, make sure you:

- Know your NCAA eligibility rules and when to declare
- Work with compliance offices before signing any deals or agents
- Understand your visa status—most F-1 student-athletes **cannot turn pro or be employed in sports** without switching to a different visa (like an O-1 or P-1 for athletes)

If you plan to go **pro in your home country**, research:

- Which leagues are open to you based on age, skill, and experience
- How your NIL earnings and U.S. competition record may be viewed
- Whether your home country has taxes or limits on foreign-earned income

If you're looking to play in **a third country** (not the U.S. or your home nation), be ready for:

- Additional paperwork (visas, work permits)
- Language or cultural adaptation
- Currency and financial planning across borders

Talk to agents, international athlete unions, or advisors who understand **sports migration laws** and eligibility.

Step 3: Build a Pro-Ready Brand

Your reputation, digital presence, and story matter—especially if you're not playing in a top-tier league.

Use your time as a student-athlete to:

- Build a clean, professional social media footprint
- Create a personal website or portfolio with your stats, highlights, and media coverage
- Tell your story in a way that resonates globally—your background, struggles, values, and goals

Coaches, sponsors, and agents will look you up. Make sure what they find **reflects your work ethic, leadership, and potential.**

Step 4: Prepare Your Finances Like a Pro—Now

Many athletes make the mistake of **starting to think about money only after the big contract comes.** But going pro isn't just about earning—it's about managing what you earn.

Start practicing now:

- Track every dollar from NIL income
- Learn how to save and invest—even small amounts
- Know how to pay taxes in multiple countries (if applicable)
- Understand budgeting during off-seasons or injury gaps

- Work with a **cross-border financial advisor** if you expect to live or earn in more than one country

Your financial literacy now can **extend or shorten your pro career**. Bad money decisions often lead athletes to retire early—or keep playing when they don't want to.

Step 5: Build Your Professional Support Team

If you're serious about going pro, you'll need more than a coach.
Start identifying:

- A **licensed agent** or sports attorney (never sign with someone without checking credentials)
- A **financial advisor** who understands athlete compensation and international taxes
- A **media or brand consultant** to help you manage your online image
- A **mentor or former pro** who's walked your path and can give real talk

Pro athletes don't succeed alone. Neither should you.

Step 6: Have a Backup Plan (Seriously)

Even if you're confident you'll make it, the smart move is to **always have a Plan B**.
Ask yourself:

- What will I do if I get injured?
- What if I don't get signed after college?
- Can I coach? Train others? Launch a business?
- Should I apply for graduate school or a work visa?

Having options doesn't mean you're giving up—it means you're prepared.

Real Talk: What the Numbers Say

Here's a snapshot from NCAA data (recent estimates):

- Less than **2% of NCAA athletes** go on to play professionally in their sport.
- Most pro contracts—especially overseas or in smaller leagues—are **short-term** and **low-paying**.
- Many international athletes supplement their income with side jobs, coaching, or sponsorships.

Success is possible. But it's **earned, not assumed.** And it requires just as much financial discipline and planning as it does talent and hustle.

Final Thoughts: Go Pro With a Plan

Whether you want to sign in the U.S., return home to play, or represent a new country abroad, one thing is clear: **The transition from college athlete to professional is a business move.**

So treat it that way.

- Know your legal options
- Handle your finances
- Build your brand
- Prepare your paperwork
- Surround yourself with people who care about *you*, not just your talent

Going pro isn't the end goal—it's the *next level* of responsibility.

You've already made it far. Now it's time to take the next step—with your eyes open, your finances tight, and your goals locked in.

Chapter 26: NIL and the Transfer Portal

Transferring schools used to be a huge decision. Now, thanks to the NCAA Transfer Portal and the rise of NIL, it's more common—and more complex—than ever. For international student-athletes, the stakes are even higher.

Yes, switching programs might give you better exposure, a bigger role, or more NIL opportunities. But it can also create **visa challenges, financial aid risks, lost eligibility, and brand instability** if you're not careful.

This chapter will help you break it down, plan it out, and protect your future if you're thinking about entering—or navigating—the transfer portal.

What Is the Transfer Portal, Really?

The NCAA Transfer Portal is a system that allows student-athletes to publicly declare their intent to transfer to another school. Once you're in the portal, other coaches can contact you, and you can explore new opportunities.

While the portal has opened up flexibility and freedom for athletes, it has also created:

- **More competition** for limited roster spots
- **Uncertainty** around scholarships and financial aid
- **Brand instability** if you've already built an NIL presence at your first school
- **Legal and immigration risks** for international athletes whose student status is tied to enrollment

What International Athletes Must Consider

If you're competing in the U.S. on an F-1 visa, transferring isn't just a school switch—it's a **legal process.**

Here's what you need to consider:

SEVIS Record and Visa Transfer

- Your **SEVIS record** (Student and Exchange Visitor Information System) must be updated and transferred properly by your current and future school's international student offices.
- There is a time limit—**you must begin classes at the new school within five months** of transferring, or risk falling out of status.
- You may need to **request a new I-20** from the new institution.

Eligibility and NCAA Requirements

- Just because you're admitted to a new school doesn't mean you're eligible to compete immediately.
- Depending on your sport and level (DI, DII, NAIA), you may need to **sit out for a year**—or you may be immediately eligible under a one-time exception.
- International athletes may also face **credit transfer problems**, affecting graduation timelines and athletic eligibility.

Scholarships and Financial Aid

- Your athletic scholarship **does not transfer automatically** to your new school.
- You must **renegotiate financial aid**—which could be more, less, or nothing.
- If your scholarship was covering housing, meals, or international student fees, ask how that will be handled at the next school.

How NIL May Be Affected By Transferring

Transferring schools can reset your NIL situation—sometimes in your favor, but not always.

Potential NIL Benefits from Transferring:

- More media exposure or playing time
- Better school-specific collectives or brand networks
- Stronger support from athletic department or city fanbase
- Opportunity to rebrand or expand your market reach

Risks and Challenges:

- NIL deals tied to your former school, coach, or local community may be voided
- Contracts with deliverables you can't fulfill (e.g., an in-person appearance at your former school) could trigger **breach of contract** penalties
- Brands may pause new deals until your playing status is clear
- Transfer rumors can affect how collectives or donors view your loyalty and future potential

Pro tip: Never sign long-term NIL deals without clear **"termination" or "transfer" clauses** that explain what happens if you switch schools.

Managing Relationships When You Transfer

Transferring isn't just a business move—it's personal. You're leaving teammates, coaches, friends, and maybe even mentors who've been part of your journey.

Here's how to handle it with professionalism:

- **Be honest but respectful.** You can want something different without tearing down what you're leaving.

- **Don't burn bridges.** You never know who will become a coach, scout, or reference later in your career.
- **Handle your NIL exit strategy.** Let brands and partners know if you're changing locations. Communicate clearly and review your agreements.

And most of all: **keep your integrity intact.** The way you leave is just as important as where you land.

Smart Questions to Ask Before You Enter the Portal

Ask yourself—and your new school—these questions first:

- Will my visa status stay active during the transfer?
- What happens to my athletic scholarship and other financial aid?
- How long will I have to sit out (if at all)?
- How does the athletic department support international athletes and NIL deals?
- What happens to my current NIL deals? Do I need to cancel or renegotiate them?
- Does the new school have resources for international tax reporting, branding, and compliance?

Final Thoughts: Transfer With Purpose

The transfer portal can be a powerful tool—but it's not a shortcut. It's a decision that deserves real thought, real research, and real conversations.

For international student-athletes, that decision has **extra layers**: immigration, finances, and brand identity.

So before you jump in, ask yourself:

- Am I running from something—or moving toward something better?
- Do I have a plan for my education, my sport, and my money?
- Have I protected my NIL interests and legal status?

If the answer is yes—you're not just transferring. You're *leveling up*.

Chapter 27: Car Chase

This is soooo random, but I've always wanted to write a book with a car chase.

Seriously—whenever someone tells me about a book they're reading—whether it's a mystery, romance, finance guide, or even a cookbook—I always ask with a grin:

"Yeah, but does it have a car chase?"

So YES, this book absolutely has a car chase.

But not the *Fast & Furious* kind.

(Although, if Vin Diesel ever wants to narrate this audiobook in four languages… call me.)

This car chase is more real than anything Hollywood can make up.

It's already happening.

You're in it.

Right now.

Because when you're an international student-athlete navigating Name, Image, and Likeness in a foreign country, every day can feel like you're flying down a highway with unfamiliar road signs, different rules, and no pit stops.

You're the Driver.

You've got talent. Visibility. Followers. Momentum.

You've come a long way from home. You've adapted. You've earned your spot.

The NIL engine is running.

Opportunities are real.

The road ahead is wide open.

But let's pull over for a second. Look at your **dashboard.**

Is Your Fuel Light On?

That's your **budget**.

Too many athletes start fast, cash a deal, and immediately blow through it—on gear, travel, tech, or even supporting family back home.

You can't run on empty—even if the exterior looks good.

Is Your Check Engine Light Flashing?

That might be the **contract you signed without reading**.

Or the **1099 form** sitting unopened in your inbox.

Or the **taxes** you didn't realize you owe in *two* countries.

Or that new friend who keeps saying, "Just one loan, bro—I'll pay you back."

Ignore these signals, and your NIL journey could stall—*fast.*

Are You Watching the Rearview Mirror?

Behind you:

- **Visa restrictions** waiting to trip you up.
- **Scammers** looking for easy targets.
- **Compliance offices** monitoring your eligibility.
- **Financial habits** from back home that might not work here.

What's behind you doesn't have to define you.

But you need to know what's chasing you before it catches you off guard.

And What About Your GPS?

Where are you headed?

Do you have a direction—or are you just taking every flashy exit that shows up in your feed?

Long-term wealth?

Financial independence?

A business that supports your community back home?

Or are you burning gas just to look good while driving in circles?

The Truth About the NIL Car Chase

This chase isn't about speed. It's about **control**.

It's about knowing when to switch lanes, when to slow down, and when to hit the gas with a strategy.

Yes, others will zoom past you—flexing fake lifestyles, making noise, grabbing attention.

But what they won't show you?

- The **breakdowns**
- The **burnouts**
- The moments they ran out of gas and had **no one to call**
- The brand deals that *vanished* after one bad post
- The visa issues that cost them their scholarship

This Book Is Your Manual

You're the one steering.

This book?

It's your **manual**.

Your **map**.

Your **legal translator, financial advisor, and cultural compass**—all in the glovebox.

Because NIL is fast.

Life in a new country is faster.

And there's no worse feeling than realizing you had the keys to your own success, but never learned how to **drive it properly**.

So yes, this book has a car chase.

But you? You're the one in control now.

Let's make sure you actually know where you're going—and that you **arrive safely, ready, and unshaken.**

Buckle up. Let's go.

Chapter 28: Content Across Borders — Creating, Collaborating, and Growing Your Brand Globally

For international student-athletes, traveling home during school breaks is an important and emotional journey. It's a time to reconnect with family, rest from the demands of the season, and recharge mentally. But for athletes navigating the Name, Image, and Likeness (NIL) space, going home isn't just about recovery — it's an opportunity to expand your brand in ways that domestic athletes might not be able to.

The unique cultural, linguistic, and geographic perspectives that international student-athletes carry make for powerful storytelling. And in the age of digital content, stories are currency. In this chapter, we're going to talk about how you can build your NIL platform while you're home, even if you're thousands of miles away from your U.S. school, sponsors, and teammates. We'll also explore how to collaborate across borders with content creators, student-athlete teammates, and brand reps to keep your name, influence, and following growing.

Why Going Home Doesn't Mean Going Quiet

Some international athletes worry that returning home for breaks or the offseason means falling off the radar. There's no media coverage, no games, fewer brand reps reaching out, and limited access to facilities. The concern is that you'll lose momentum, visibility, and brand value.

But here's the truth: momentum doesn't come from geography. It comes from consistency. It comes from your ability to stay relevant and visible, even when you're away from the action. Going home is not a break from NIL — it's a chance to be strategic about showing your full story.

Think about it: most domestic athletes are sharing similar content — gym sessions, game clips, locker room photos. You have the opportunity to offer something different. Something international. Something personal. And brands are looking for that.

What Kind of Content Should You Create While Home?

Rule of Thumb #1: Show what makes you different.

Your hometown, your language, your family dynamic, your community — these are all things most American college athletes can't replicate. Use that to your advantage. Think about creating content that reflects:

- Your journey: Share where you started, who supported you, and what obstacles you overcame.
- Your training: Show how you stay in shape with the resources available at home.
- Your culture: Highlight local food, music, traditions, or routines.
- Your roots: Tell stories about how sports shaped your childhood or how your country views your sport.

Example: A track athlete from Kenya films a video running through the countryside where they first learned to sprint. They speak in both Swahili and English, talking about how their village helped fund their plane ticket to the U.S. That video goes viral and catches the attention of a global athletic brand looking to expand in East Africa.

Rule of Thumb #2: Be consistent, even if production is basic.

You don't need studio lighting or a campus film crew to make engaging content. A smartphone, good lighting, and honest storytelling are enough. Post regularly. Show up on your platforms. Engage with your audience.

Collaborating with U.S.-Based Creators and Teammates While Abroad

Just because you're home doesn't mean you're disconnected. In fact, your U.S.-based teammates, student media creators, and influencers might be looking for ways to keep their own content fresh. This is where you can build bridges and co-create.

Rule of Thumb #3: Keep your creative network warm.

Before leaving campus, talk to your teammates, videographers, and brand reps. Let them know you want to collaborate over break. Some ideas include:

- Split-screen workout challenges
- Video interviews or podcasts over Zoom
- "Pass the ball" content chains where each athlete films a short clip and edits them into a sequence
- Co-branded giveaways that highlight both your country and your U.S. campus

Example: A volleyball player from Brazil co-creates a TikTok dance trend with teammates still on campus. They each film their segments, edit them into one video, and tag each other. It trends on both American and Brazilian social platforms, leading to new followers and interest from a bilingual lifestyle brand.

Rule of Thumb #4: Think beyond sports clips.

Brands love versatility. Collaborate on content that isn't just about athletic performance. Try:

- Study routines
- Mental health practices
- Nutrition habits in your home country
- Day-in-the-life content
- Your travel experiences going to and from school

The more human and relatable your content is, the more likely people will engage — and the more attractive you become to sponsors looking for global representation.

Growing Your Audience Across Cultures

Being international means you have access to two (or more) different audiences. You have your American followers and your audience back home. Your content should speak to both — even if not every post does it equally.

Rule of Thumb #5: Use bilingual content when possible.

Subtitles, dual-language captions, or even switching between languages within a video can help you connect more broadly. Use your native language to build loyalty with fans from home, and English to stay accessible to your U.S. audience and sponsors.

Example: A Turkish basketball player hosts a live Q&A in both Turkish and English. They pin a translator comment in the chat and repeat key points in both languages. The result? A boost in engagement and positive feedback from both audiences.

Rule of Thumb #6: Tell stories that cross cultural lines.

The more your content reflects universal values — like family, perseverance, identity, humor, growth — the easier it will resonate worldwide. Let your life, not just your sport, be the content.

Leveraging Brand and School Media While Abroad

Rule of Thumb #7: Ask for your content before you leave.

Most athletic departments have tons of footage from games, practices, and photo shoots. Before you head home for a break, request access to:

- Game clips
- Headshots and photos
- B-roll or behind-the-scenes footage

Use this content to stay active on social media even when you're not physically on campus.

Example: A soccer player from South Korea posts a series called "Flashback Fridays," where each week they post a photo or video from the season with a short personal reflection in Korean and English. It becomes a consistent anchor in their feed.

Rule of Thumb #8: Share your school's brand abroad.

Tag your university and athletic program in content filmed at home. This helps keep your visibility alive within the program and shows you're still engaged. It may also lead to your content being reshared on official platforms, which boosts your credibility and reach.

NIL Considerations When Earning or Promoting from Abroad

It's not just about creating content — it's about doing it right. International athletes must be careful with how they earn and promote during breaks, especially when outside the U.S.

Rule of Thumb #9: If you're earning money, make sure it's legal.

Depending on your visa, certain types of work or compensation abroad may be subject to both U.S. and local laws. Always:

- Keep NIL activity documented
- Use U.S.-based bank accounts for payment (when possible)
- Consult with school compliance or a visa advisor if you're unsure

Rule of Thumb #10: Separate "branding" from "work."

Creating content to maintain and grow your brand is generally allowed. Signing paid contracts while abroad requires more scrutiny. When in doubt, treat content creation as brand building unless a professional advisor confirms otherwise.

Planning Ahead: Your Global Content Calendar

Here's how to stay consistent while you're home:

1. **Week 1** – Welcome home video: Reintroduce yourself to your audience. Share your goals for break.
2. **Week 2** – Hometown highlight: A short vlog or montage about where you're from.
3. **Week 3** – Training or discipline-focused post: Show how you're staying prepared.
4. **Week 4** – Collaboration: Post with a friend, creator, or teammate (even virtually).
5. **Week 5** – Community spotlight: Film something with a local school, team, or fan base.
6. **Week 6** – Reflective story: Share how your perspective has changed between the U.S. and home.
7. **Week 7** – Travel tips or cultural crossover content: Teach something new to your audience.

Stick to a rhythm that works for you. The point isn't to flood your feed. It's to show consistency, intention, and growth.

Final Thoughts: You Are the Bridge

As an international student-athlete, you're not just a competitor. You're a cultural connector. A bilingual brand. A walking global story.

Going home doesn't mean falling behind. It means expanding your brand beyond borders.

So create. Collaborate. Show your world. And make sure every piece of content adds depth to the story you're building, not just likes to a feed.

This is what smart NIL looks like. This is how you stay in the race while staying true to yourself.

The world is watching. Show them who you really are.

Chapter 29: How Investing Works – Making Your Money Work While You Train

As an international student-athlete, you're used to putting in the work—early lifts, long practices, late nights studying. You know what it means to grind. But here's a secret most athletes aren't taught: **your money can work just as hard as you do.**

That's what **investing** is all about. It's not about being rich. It's not about being a finance major. It's about learning how to **grow the money you already have** over time so you're not just playing to survive—you're building for something bigger.

In this chapter, we'll break down how investing works, why it matters, and how you can start—even if you're new, unsure, or working with a small budget.

What Is Investing, Really?

Investing simply means putting your money into something that has the potential to grow in value over time.

When you invest, you're using your money to buy something—like a stock, a piece of a company (share), or a fund—that could be worth more in the future. You're trading today's dollars for the chance to have more dollars tomorrow. It's the opposite of spending. It's planting a seed, not eating the fruit.

How Does Money Grow?

There are two main ways your money can grow when you invest:

1. **Capital Gains** – When you buy something at one price and sell it later at a higher price. For example, buying a stock at $50 and selling it at $70 earns you a $20 profit.
2. **Dividends** – Some companies share their profits with investors by paying you small amounts of money (called dividends) every few months—just for owning their stock.

Over time, many investments also benefit from **compound growth**—meaning you earn money not just on what you invested, but also on the money it already made. It's like building muscle. The stronger you get, the faster you can grow stronger.

Common Types of Investments

There are lots of ways to invest, but here are the most common ones you'll hear about:

- **Stocks:** You own a piece of a company. High risk, high potential reward.
- **Bonds:** You're loaning money to a company or government. Lower risk, but also lower reward.
- **Mutual Funds:** A group of stocks or bonds managed by a professional. Diversified, meaning your risk is spread out.
- **ETFs (Exchange-Traded Funds):** Similar to mutual funds, but easier to buy and sell like a stock. Often a great starting point for beginners.
- **Index Funds:** A type of ETF or mutual fund that follows a market index (like the S&P 500). These are simple, low-cost, and proven over time.

Why Should Student-Athletes Care About Investing?

You might be thinking: *"Why invest now? I'm just trying to get through school."* Here's why investing matters—even now:

- **Time is your biggest advantage.** Starting young gives your money more years to grow.
- **NIL earnings won't last forever.** Invest part of it now so you don't spend it all.
- **Athletic careers aren't guaranteed.** An injury can change your path. Investments give you options.
- **It builds discipline.** Just like training, it's about doing the work consistently—even when no one's watching.

How Much Do You Need to Start?

You don't need thousands. Some investment apps let you start with **$5 to $50**. The point is not how much you start with—it's that you **start at all.** Think of your early investments like reps in the gym. They build habits, even if they're small.

How to Actually Start Investing

Here's a simple roadmap:

1. **Open a brokerage account** (like with Fidelity, Charles Schwab, or Vanguard). Some platforms like Robinhood or M1 Finance are beginner-friendly, but make sure they work with your visa and legal status.
2. **Transfer money from your U.S. bank account.**
3. **Buy ETFs or index funds** (like S&P 500 or Total Market funds) to get started. They're diversified, affordable, and a good way to learn.
4. **Check your account once in a while—but don't stress about daily**

ups and downs. Investing is long-term.

What About IRAs and Roth IRAs?

As discussed in a previous chapter, international students may not qualify for these U.S. retirement accounts unless you have a Social Security Number (SSN) and taxable income.

- **Traditional IRA** – You may be able to deduct contributions now and pay taxes later when you withdraw in retirement.
- **Roth IRA** – You pay taxes now, but the money grows tax-free and comes out tax-free in retirement.

If you qualify, a **Roth IRA** is one of the most powerful tools for young athletes, because it grows over decades—tax-free. But if you can't open one yet, that's okay. Start with a taxable investment account, and switch later if your situation changes.

Staying Safe: Smart Investing Tips

- **Avoid the hype.** Just because a friend made money on crypto doesn't mean you should jump in.
- **Don't invest what you can't afford to lose.** Keep enough in your bank account for everyday life.
- **Diversify.** Don't put all your money in one stock, brand, or influencer tip.
- **Use automatic contributions.** Many platforms let you invest a little each month without thinking about it.
- **Be patient.** Investing is not a get-rich-quick game—it's about staying in the game long enough to win.

Common Mistakes First-Time Investors Make

- **Trying to time the market** – Nobody knows the perfect time to buy or sell.
- **Getting emotional when the market dips** – Stay calm and think long-term.
- **Following social media hype** – Not all "advice" is good advice.
- **Investing everything and leaving nothing in cash** – Always have an emergency fund.

Final Thoughts: Play the Long Game

As an athlete, you know how much work goes into improving over time. Investing works the same way. It takes discipline, consistency, and a willingness to be uncomfortable at first. But when you do it right—and start early—it can change your life.

Whether you're investing $20 or $2,000, you're sending a message to your future self: *I believe in you, and I'm building for you today.*

So make your money run sprints while you recover. Make it lift while you sleep. That's how investing works.

And you're ready for it.

Chapter 30: You Love Them. But You Can't Save Them All.

Let's talk about one of the hardest parts of coming into money—especially NIL money—when you're young, far from home, and possibly the first in your family to earn at this level.

Helping a single mom back home who worked multiple jobs to support your dream? You want to.

Helping your dad who never had much but made sure you got to training? Feels like the least you can do.

Supporting a friend or cousin who stuck by you when no one else did? It seems only right.

You want to be generous.

You want to show appreciation.

You want to prove you're not "too big to care."

But here's the truth: if you're not careful, you'll drown while trying to carry everyone else.

This chapter is about how to do it differently—how to help without hurting yourself, how to give without guilt, and how to protect your future so you're not stuck saying, "I used to have money..."

Start With This Truth: You Are Not Their Retirement Plan

When you're the first in your family—or your village or community—to "make it," people will naturally look to you for support. Sometimes they'll ask directly. Other times, they'll expect it silently. In some cultures, supporting family isn't optional—it's assumed.

But even if you choose to help, you need a structure. Otherwise, emotional decisions can lead to financial chaos.

You are not your family's emergency fund.

You are not your community's bank.

You are not a bottomless pit of money.

You may be earning NIL income now—but if you want it to last, you need to build boundaries.

Option 1: The Monthly Budget Strategy

Let's say you want to help consistently—maybe with groceries, school fees, or rent for your family.

Instead of saying yes every time someone reaches out, set a monthly family support budget.

Example: You decide you can afford to send $500/month without sacrificing your own savings, investment, or visa-related compliance.

You break it down like this:

- $200 to cover groceries or utilities
- $200 to pay tuition or rent (directly to the provider)
- $100 for flexible needs via prepaid card or remittance

Once that $500 is spent, that's it for the month.

If someone asks for more, you say:

"I've already reached my family support budget this month. I'll see what I can do next month, but I can't go over it."

That's not being cold—it's being consistent.

Option 2: The Lump Sum Strategy

Maybe you'd rather avoid the monthly stress altogether. Instead, you decide to give a one-time gift upfront—and make it clear it's not ongoing.

Example: You receive a $20,000 NIL deal and choose to send $2,000 to help cover your mom's debt or help your dad fix the house.

You say:

"This is a one-time gift. I wanted to do something meaningful, but after this, I won't be able to send more for now."

Then you stick to it. You don't follow up with more money unless you choose to later.

This is not a subscription—it's a gift with boundaries.

If You're Helping Multiple People

Maybe your parents both need help. Maybe you've got siblings, cousins, or even childhood teammates reaching out. Same rules apply.

Set a total support budget and divide it.

Example: You commit to $6,000/year, or $500/month total.

You decide:

- Mom gets $300
- Dad gets $100
- One other relative or friend gets $100

That's your cap. You don't add more, and you don't shuffle money around if someone's situation suddenly "gets worse." Your plan comes first. Everyone else fits inside that plan—or not at all.

Say It Early. Say It Often.

If you don't explain how much and how often you're able to help, people will assume the limit doesn't exist.

And that's where resentment and entitlement grow.

It might feel awkward, especially across cultural lines, but it's necessary.

You say:

"I love you, and I'm proud to be in a position to help. But I've set a monthly limit on what I can give. Once that number is reached, I can't go beyond it. I'm doing this to protect my future—not because I don't care."

And when they say:

"Just this once..."

You hold the line.

Boundaries are not disrespectful. They are the most respectful way to love someone *without* losing yourself.

How to Avoid Enabling

Sometimes helping becomes enabling. Here's how you know it's gone too far:

- They stop trying to help themselves
- They start expecting you to provide
- They make you feel guilty when you say no
- You keep giving money for the same problem, over and over
- You feel resentment building inside

Here's how to help without enabling:

- Pay bills directly (not through someone else)
- Offer help with job training or school—not just cash
- Share financial literacy resources (yes, even this book)
- Make your help temporary, not indefinite

If they need $200 for rent every month, what they really need isn't another $200—they need a *plan*.

You can love someone without being their financial crutch.

If They Get Upset, That's Okay

People may not like your new boundaries—especially if they're used to you always saying yes.

They may say:

"You've changed."

"You forgot where you came from."

"You're selfish."

Let them say it.

Because the goal isn't to win everyone's approval. The goal is to build something that lasts—so you can help them the *right* way, not the reactive way.

You can't pour into others if your cup is empty. You can't carry your entire community on a financial back that's still under construction.

Final Thoughts: Help With Strategy, Not Emotion

You are not heartless for saying no.

You are not selfish for setting limits.

You are not wrong for wanting to protect what you've earned.

If you choose to help, do it:

- With intention
- With a clear budget
- With firm boundaries
- Without shame

Because the best thing you can give your family or community isn't just a check.

It's an *example*.

Of discipline.

Of long-term thinking.

Of what building real wealth looks like.

If they love you, they'll understand.

And if they don't now?

They will, when you're still standing strong ten years from now—while others are broke, bitter, and still wondering what happened to all the money.

That's not selfish.

That's real love.

That's leadership.

That's legacy.

Chapter 31: What Is the Market, the Economy, and Everything Else You See on TV?

You've probably heard things like:

"The market is crashing."

"The S&P 500 is on a hot streak."

"The Fed raised interest rates again."

"Inflation is out of control."

If you're an international student-athlete, it might all sound overwhelming—especially when you're already navigating a new country, a new culture, and the complexities of NIL. But here's the truth: the stock market is just another game. It has teams, scores, momentum shifts, rules, strategies, and yes, even a few surprise injuries.

Once you learn the rules, you'll stop reacting—and start planning. You'll see that investing is a tool that can help you turn short-term NIL income into long-term financial success.

Let's break it down so you can start playing to win.

What Exactly Is the Stock Market?

The stock market is where people buy and sell shares of companies. When you buy a share, you own a small piece of that company—like Nike, Apple, or Amazon.

Sports analogy: It's like being part of a sports franchise. You're not just cheering from the sidelines—you're part of the ownership team. If the team does well and gains value, your share becomes more valuable too.

What Causes the Market to Go Up or Down?

The stock market moves based on supply and demand. If more people want to buy a stock, the price goes up. If more people want to sell, the price drops.

What affects that supply and demand? News, earnings reports, global events, political changes, interest rate decisions, and even social media.

Sports analogy: It's like player hype. If an athlete performs well, their stock rises. If there's an injury or scandal, it drops.

What's the Difference Between the Stock Market and the Economy?

The market is a scoreboard—it reflects what investors *expect* will happen. The economy is the actual game—jobs, production, consumer spending, and trade.

Sports analogy: Think of the stock market like fantasy football. It's based on projections and predictions. The real economy is the actual football game. Sometimes they match up, and sometimes they don't.

Is the Market Risky? Can I Lose All My Money?

Yes, there's always risk in investing. If you put all your money into one stock, it could crash and you could lose a lot.

But if you spread your money across hundreds of companies—like in an index fund or an ETF (Exchange-Traded Fund)—your risk is much lower.

Sports analogy: Betting on one player to carry the whole team is risky. But building a strong, balanced team gives you a much better shot at winning.

What's the Best Way to Start Investing?

For most people, the smartest strategy is:

- Invest in low-cost index funds or ETFs
- Use a Roth IRA or brokerage account (depending on visa restrictions and residency status)
- Focus on the long term
- Stay consistent, no matter what the market is doing

Sports analogy: It's like running the same high-percentage play over and over. It may not be flashy, but it wins games.

When's the Best Time to Start?

Now. Always now. The earlier you begin, the more your money can grow.

Sports analogy: The best athletes don't wait for playoffs to start training. They put in the work during the offseason. Early investing builds long-term strength.

What's the S&P 500?

It's a list of the 500 largest companies in the U.S. and is often used to measure how the stock market is doing overall.

Sports analogy: Think of it like the AP Top 25 rankings for business. If most of those 500 companies are doing well, the market is usually performing well too.

What's a Bull Market vs. a Bear Market?

Bull Market = prices rising, investors confident

Bear Market = prices falling 20% or more, investors fearful

Sports analogy: A bull market is like a winning streak. A bear market is a losing streak. Either way, the season isn't over—you just adjust your strategy.

Should I Sell When the Market Drops?

No. Selling during a drop locks in your losses. Markets recover—but only if you stay in the game.

Sports analogy: You don't pull your best player after one bad quarter. You stay the course and play the full game.

How Much Money Do I Need to Start?

You can start investing with $50, $100, or whatever you can afford. Many platforms allow you to buy fractional shares of big stocks.

Sports analogy: You don't have to start as the star. Just get on the roster. Show up. Do the reps.

Can I Make Fast Money in the Market?

Sometimes. But short-term wins are gambling, not investing. Day trading is risky. Most people lose money doing it.

Sports analogy: Anyone can hit a half-court shot once. Champions win by making consistent layups and smart plays.

What's an ETF?

An Exchange-Traded Fund is a basket of investments—stocks, bonds, or both—that you can buy or sell like a single stock. It gives you instant diversification.

Sports analogy: It's like drafting an entire starting lineup in one move instead of betting on one player to carry the team.

Is Investing Only for Rich People?

Not at all. Investing is for *anyone* who wants to build wealth. You don't need to start big—you just need to start.

Sports analogy: Great careers start in high school gyms, not pro arenas. What matters is putting in the work now.

What's the Difference Between a Stock and a Bond?

A stock means you own part of a company.

A bond means you loan money to a company or government and they promise to pay you back with interest.

Stocks tend to grow faster but are riskier. Bonds are more stable but grow slower.

Sports analogy: Stocks are like high-scoring forwards. Bonds are like defenders—steady and reliable.

What's Diversification?

Diversification means spreading your money across many types of investments so you're not dependent on just one.

Sports analogy: You don't build a team with only point guards. You need a balance of roles—offense, defense, speed, experience.

Why Do People Say "Buy Low, Sell High"?

Because the goal is to buy investments when they're cheap and sell when they're worth more.

But most people panic and do the opposite. They buy when prices are high and sell when things go down.

Sports analogy: You don't bench your star player after one cold streak. You trust them to recover and play the long game.

How Do I Know What to Invest In?

Start simple. Focus on:

- S&P 500 index funds
- Total market ETFs
- Low-cost, diversified options
- Reinvesting dividends
- Staying consistent

Sports analogy: You don't need trick plays. Just stick to what works. Fundamentals win games.

What Happens in a Recession?

A recession is when the economy slows down—fewer jobs, less spending, and cautious business activity. The market may drop during this time.

Sports analogy: A recession is like a rebuilding season. You might not win it all this year, but you reset, train, and come back stronger.

Do I Need a Financial Advisor?

Not to start. You can use apps like:

- Fidelity
- Vanguard
- Schwab
- M1 Finance
- Public
- Betterment

But as your NIL income grows, or your financial situation gets more complex, it's smart to bring in a professional advisor—someone who can act as your financial coach.

What's the #1 Rule of Investing?

Start early. Stay consistent. Don't panic.

Sports analogy: The best players aren't perfect—they're dependable. They follow the plan, train every day, and don't get rattled by one bad game.

What's a Dividend?

Some companies pay a portion of their profits to shareholders. That's called a dividend.

Sports analogy: It's like getting a bonus for simply being on the team—even if you're not playing right now.

How Often Should I Check My Investments?

Once a month. Maybe once a quarter. Don't obsess.

Sports analogy: Constantly checking your account is like staring at the scoreboard during warm-ups. Focus on training, not tracking every point.

What's a Stock Split?

When a company's stock gets expensive, it might split into more shares at a lower price. The value stays the same—you just own more shares.

Sports analogy: It's like changing your jersey number. The look changes, but your role on the team stays the same.

What's a Market Correction?

When the market drops about 10% from a recent high, that's a correction. It's normal and healthy.

Sports analogy: A correction is like a timeout after a rough quarter—not a crisis. Just a chance to regroup.

Should I Invest if the Market Is Going Down?

Yes. That's when prices are discounted.

Sports analogy: It's like getting your favorite gear at 30% off. Still the same value—just a better deal.

Can I Lose All My Money in the Market?

If you put it all in one stock? Yes.

If you diversify with index funds or ETFs? Very unlikely. Markets dip, but history shows they bounce back over time.

Sports analogy: One player can go down. But a strong bench keeps your season alive.

What's a Mutual Fund vs. an ETF?

Both hold collections of investments.

- Mutual funds trade once per day and may have higher fees.
- ETFs trade all day like stocks and are usually cheaper and more flexible.

Most beginners start with ETFs.

Sports analogy: Mutual funds are like traditional coaches—dependable but slower. ETFs are today's fast-paced game plan—efficient and adaptable.

What Are Interest Rates and Why Do They Matter?

Interest rates are the cost of borrowing money. When rates go up, loans cost more and spending slows. That can cause the stock market to drop.

Sports analogy: It's like when your coach makes you run extra sprints. It slows things down—but builds long-term discipline.

What's Dollar-Cost Averaging?

It means investing the same amount of money at regular intervals—no matter what the market is doing.

Example: $200/month into an ETF.

This lets you buy more shares when prices are low and fewer when prices are high, averaging your cost over time.

Sports analogy: It's like lifting weights every week—whether you feel strong or not. Discipline beats emotion.

Final Thoughts: Master the System. Don't Just Play in It.

The financial world isn't a mystery. It's a system. One you can learn. One you can win.

- Diversify your portfolio like you build a team
- Train your money like you train your body
- Stay in the game—even when it gets tough
- Don't fall for hype or panic
- Invest like someone who plans to be successful for decades

Because NIL money isn't just for now. It's the seed. You decide if it grows.

Invest early. Invest smart. Build a future that goes way beyond the highlight reel.

Chapter 32: How to Start Investing – Your NIL Playbook for Building Wealth

Introduction: Don't Just Get Paid. Build Something With It.

You just landed your first big NIL deal. Maybe it's $1,000. Maybe it's $100,000. Either way, the urge to celebrate is real. Buy the sneakers. Book the flight. Show love to your family back home.

But the real flex?

Financial security. Long-term wealth. Letting your money make more money.

That's what investing is all about—and the earlier you start, the stronger your financial game becomes. This chapter will walk you through what investing actually means, the types of accounts available to you, and how to turn even your first NIL check into a foundation for the future.

Step 1: Understand What Investing Actually Is

Investing is simply putting your money to work so it can grow over time.

Instead of letting your earnings sit in a checking account (or spending it all on clothes, travel, or takeout), you can invest in assets—stocks, bonds, ETFs, or mutual funds—that rise in value and pay you back over time. The more consistent you are, the more your money multiplies.

That's the power of compound interest. Even small, consistent contributions can grow into something big.

Step 2: Know Your Goals and Timeline

Before you invest, ask yourself:

- When will I need this money?
- Can I handle it going up and down in the short term?
- Am I building wealth slowly, or trying to flip money fast?

If you don't need the money for at least five years, investing is usually a smart move. If you'll need it sooner—like for tuition, travel, or emergencies—it's better to keep that portion in cash.

Step 3: Choose Your Investment Account

Not all investment accounts are created equal. Each has its own rules, tax benefits, and accessibility—especially for international students, where visa status can limit account eligibility.

Roth IRA

- Funded with after-tax money
- Grows tax-free
- Withdrawals in retirement are tax-free
- Contribution limit (2025): $6,500
- Must have earned income (not from scholarships or stipends)

Why it's great:

If your NIL income qualifies as "earned income" under IRS rules and your visa status permits it, a Roth IRA is one of the best long-term tools. You're likely in a low tax bracket now, so paying taxes upfront lets you avoid them later—forever.

Note: Check with a tax advisor to make sure your visa status allows IRA contributions. Not all F-1 students can legally contribute.

Traditional IRA

- May allow a tax deduction now
- Grows tax-deferred
- Taxes are paid when withdrawn later
- Same contribution limit: $6,500
- Income restrictions may apply

Best for: Athletes who qualify for a deduction now and expect to be in a lower tax bracket at retirement. Like the Roth IRA, visa status and earned income rules apply.

Taxable Brokerage Account

- No contribution limits or income caps
- Taxed on dividends and gains
- Full flexibility—you can access it at any time

Best for: Any athlete, regardless of visa, looking to invest money they don't need immediately. No age, income, or citizenship barriers. Great for long-term growth and short-term access.

SEP IRA (Simplified Employee Pension)

- For self-employed athletes running their NIL brand like a business
- Contribute up to 25% of earnings, up to $66,000 (2025 limit)
- Tax-deductible contributions
- Grows tax-deferred

Best for: High-earning international athletes operating under an LLC or as sole proprietors. *Again, check visa and tax rules before setting this up.*

SIMPLE IRA

- Primarily for small business owners with employees
- Contribution limit: $16,000 plus employer match
- Grows tax-deferred

Best for: International athletes who launch a brand or agency and hire others. This is less common for college students, but worth knowing about.

Step 4: The $100,000 NIL Check — Sample Breakdown

Let's say you just got a $100,000 NIL check. It's exciting—but it comes with responsibility. Here's a smart way to break it down:

Step 1: Set Aside Taxes

Unless taxes were withheld from your payment, assume roughly 30% will be owed in federal, state, and self-employment taxes.

- $100,000 × 30% = **$30,000 for taxes**
- Keep this money in a separate savings account—do *not* touch it. Taxes hit harder when you're not prepared.

Step 2: Fund a Roth IRA

Assuming you're eligible based on income and visa status:

- Max Roth IRA contribution: **$6,500**
- Invest in a low-cost index fund (like an S&P 500 fund) that tracks the U.S. stock market. That money will grow tax-free for decades.

Step 3: Invest in a Taxable Brokerage Account

With the Roth maxed out, keep building your investment portfolio.

- Contribute **$30,000–$40,000**
- Use diversified ETFs or index funds. This is flexible and accessible before retirement if needed.

Step 4: Keep Some Cash on Hand

Life happens. Visa renewals, travel costs, injuries, or emergencies can show up at any time.

- Set aside **$10,000–$15,000**
- Keep this in a high-yield savings account or money market account. This is your safety net.

Step 5: Reward Yourself (Wisely)

You worked hard—celebrating isn't wrong. Just do it with a cap.

- Spend **$5,000–$10,000**
- Use it for a trip, some gear, or something meaningful. Enjoy it without guilt—but don't let lifestyle creep drain your future.

Recap of the $100K Game Plan

- **$30,000** – Taxes
- **$6,500** – Roth IRA (if eligible)
- **$35,000** – Taxable investments
- **$15,000** – Emergency fund
- **$8,500** – Celebration

This is how you turn one deal into long-term power. You celebrated *and* protected your future. That's how professionals handle money.

Step 5: Set It and Stay Consistent

Even if you don't have a $100,000 deal, this approach still works.

- Save for taxes
- Invest what you can
- Build your emergency fund
- Budget your spending
- Stay consistent

Set up automatic transfers. Use simple ETFs. Reinvest dividends. Stick to your plan even when the headlines get scary.

Final Thoughts: Don't Let a One-Time Check Be Your Only Win

NIL can change your life—but only if you treat it like the *start,* not the finish.

Start now—even if it's just $100 a month. The earlier you begin, the more your money can work while you focus on school, sport, and life.

Wealth isn't about being rich today. It's about owning your tomorrow. It's about building something that lasts long after the lights go out and the seasons change.

Let your money work behind the scenes while you're grinding up front.

Because the goal isn't just to get paid.

It's to stay paid.

And that's how you build a legacy.

Chapter 33: Wrong Examples

Here are several **real-world examples of athletes who made millions and then lost it all (or most of it)** due to poor financial decisions, lack of guidance, or unsustainable lifestyles. These stories can serve as powerful teaching tools in your book or workshops to show the importance of planning, saying "no," and building wealth the right way.

1. Allen Iverson – NBA

Estimated career earnings: Over $200 million

What happened: Lavish spending, generosity to friends and family, and a divorce drained his bank account. He was known for flying his crew on private jets, buying dozens of cars, and spending tens of thousands at a time in malls. He once reportedly refused to fly commercial—even for one night.

How he bounced back: Fortunately, Reebok had a **$32 million trust** set aside for him that he can access at age 55. That move likely saved his financial future.

2. Antoine Walker – NBA

Estimated career earnings: $108 million

What happened: Walker invested in failed real estate deals, supported over 70 friends and family members, and lived a high-spending lifestyle with luxury cars, jewelry, and gambling. He filed for bankruptcy just two years after retiring.

Lesson: Even $100 million isn't enough if you don't set boundaries and manage wisely.

3. Vince Young – NFL

Estimated career earnings: Around $35 million

What happened: Young famously spent $5,000 a week at The Cheesecake Factory and once bought every seat on a Southwest Airlines flight—just so he could fly alone. He trusted the wrong people, didn't track spending, and filed for bankruptcy in 2014.

4. Delonte West – NBA

Estimated career earnings: $16 million

What happened: After a solid NBA career, West faced mental health struggles and poor financial decisions. At one point, he was seen homeless and panhandling. His story is heartbreaking and reminds us that financial literacy and mental health go hand in hand.

Current status: With support from former teammate Mark Cuban, West entered rehab and has been working to rebuild his life.

5. Bernie Kosar – NFL

Estimated career earnings: Over $20 million

What happened: Kosar tried to help too many people. He once said he had **60 checking accounts** and over **50 real estate partnerships**, most of which failed. He gave away money without structure and later filed for bankruptcy.

Lesson: You can't save everyone. If you're everyone's emergency fund, you'll go broke trying to play hero.

6. Lenny Dykstra – MLB

Estimated career earnings: $36 million

What happened: After retirement, Dykstra lived lavishly and pursued risky business ventures with borrowed money. He declared bankruptcy in 2009 and was later sentenced to prison for bankruptcy fraud and money laundering.

Lesson: Taking financial risks without a plan can cost you more than just money—it can take your freedom.

7. Mike Tyson – Boxing

Estimated career earnings: $400+ million

What happened: Lavish spending on mansions, exotic animals (he once owned three Bengal tigers), luxury cars, and a massive entourage led Tyson to bankruptcy in 2003. He admitted to spending **$1 million per month at one point**.

Current status: Tyson has made a successful comeback through podcasting, entertainment, and cannabis ventures.

Lesson: It's not about how much you make—it's how much you keep.

8. JaMarcus Russell – NFL

Estimated career earnings: $40 million

What happened: Russell signed one of the biggest rookie contracts in NFL history but had little structure or financial discipline. He reportedly spent heavily on jewelry, cars, and poor investments. He never became a consistent starter, and his money didn't last.

Lesson: Earning potential doesn't matter if you don't have a financial game plan.

9. Sheryl Swoopes – WNBA

Estimated career earnings: Millions through salary and endorsements

What happened: Despite being a pioneer in women's basketball, Swoopes filed for bankruptcy in 2004. She made poor investment decisions, including trusting the wrong advisors and business ventures that failed.

Lesson: Even trailblazers need financial education and trusted guidance.

10. Evander Holyfield – Boxing

Estimated career earnings: Over $200 million

What happened: Holyfield bought a 109-room mansion, fathered 11 children with multiple women (with huge child support obligations), and had extravagant spending habits. He lost his home to foreclosure and faced serious financial setbacks.

Lesson: Lifestyle inflation and unchecked generosity can drain even the biggest bank accounts.

Final Thoughts

These examples aren't just cautionary tales—they're reminders of how fast money can disappear without a plan. Whether you're earning $10K or $10 million from NIL deals, you need:

- A budget
- A plan
- Financial boundaries
- Trusted advisors
- A long-term mindset

Learn from their mistakes—so your story can be one of legacy, not loss.

Chapter 34: What's a Portfolio? Build Your Game Plan, Diversify Your Lineup

Every International Student-Athlete Needs a Financial Game Plan

Your athletic journey didn't happen by accident. You trained. You prepared. You studied film. You followed a plan. Now you're playing in the U.S., balancing school, sport, and (for the first time) money from NIL.

So let's ask a question:

Would you hit the field or court without a playbook? Without a strategy? Without knowing your teammates' roles?

Of course not.

That's exactly what your financial future needs—a playbook. A system. A game plan built to win over time.

Your investment portfolio is that playbook. It's a team of financial players—each with a job to do. Some score fast. Some protect the lead. Some stay ready on the bench.

If you build your portfolio wisely, you'll give yourself the best shot at financial success, not just this season—but for life.

What's in a Portfolio?

A portfolio is the collection of investments you own. It's your financial roster—diverse, strategic, and designed to work together.

Here's what might be on that roster:

- **Stocks** – Your offensive players. They can score big (grow in value), but they can also miss shots (drop in price).
- **Bonds** – Your defenders. Steady and dependable. They don't score much, but they keep you in the game.
- **Cash** – Your bench. Not flashy, but always ready when you need quick access.
- **ETFs and Mutual Funds** – Your utility players. These bundle multiple assets, offering both flexibility and teamwork.
- **Real Estate (optional)** – Your long-game strategy. Not always available to international students, but worth knowing about down the line.

Just like no coach builds a team with only scorers, your portfolio shouldn't be made of one kind of asset. You need **diversification**—a mix of different investments—to give yourself the best chance at winning through market ups and downs.

Why Diversification Matters—Especially for You

When you put all your NIL income into one investment (say, a single company's stock or one type of crypto), you're betting the entire season on one player. If they get injured—or in this case, if that investment drops—you're stuck.

Diversification means you're spreading the risk. It's like having a full team with scorers, defenders, and role players. When one investment underperforms, another can step up.

For international athletes, this matters even more. You may be helping family back home, dealing with currency exchange issues, or trying to grow wealth on a student visa. Diversification gives you stability in an unstable world.

Conservative, Moderate, and Aggressive Portfolios

Not every athlete plays the same. Some go all-in. Others play smart and steady. Your investment style should match your goals, your personality, and your timeline.

Conservative Portfolio – Play Safe

This is your defense-first strategy. Mostly bonds and cash. Very few high-risk plays. It's built to protect money—not grow it fast.

Best for:

- Athletes who might need the money soon
- Those sending money home regularly
- Anyone who's anxious about big losses

Pros:

- Less volatility
- More peace of mind
- Great for short-term needs

Cons:

- Limited growth
- Might not keep up with inflation
- Not ideal for young athletes with long-term goals

Moderate Portfolio – Balanced Game

This is your two-way team. A mix of stocks and bonds. It grows over time but doesn't go wild during market swings.

Best for:

- Athletes with 5–10 year goals
- Those who want growth but still need some protection
- People in the middle of their career or education

Pros:

- Balanced performance
- Handles ups and downs well
- Great for long-term planning with some flexibility

Cons:

- Slower growth than aggressive portfolios
- Still risky if you need cash soon
- Requires patience during slow stretches

Aggressive Portfolio – Go For It

This strategy is all about growth. Mostly stocks, minimal bonds. Big swings. Big potential. Not for the faint of heart.

Best for:

- Young athletes (under 30)
- Those who won't need the money for 10+ years
- Players who can handle emotional ups and downs

Pros:

- Highest long-term return potential
- Great for early-stage wealth building
- Takes full advantage of time and compounding

Cons:

- Big drops during market crashes
- Emotionally harder to stick with
- Not for short-term financial goals

How to Choose Your Strategy as an International Student-Athlete

This part is personal. You have to ask yourself:

- Am I sending money home regularly?
- Will I need this money before graduation?
- How stable is my visa and work eligibility?
- Can I emotionally handle watching the market go up and down?

If you're unsure, a **moderate portfolio** is usually a smart place to start. You can always shift later as your situation changes.

Be **aggressive** if:

- You're young
- You don't need the money soon
- You have other emergency savings
- You want long-term growth

Be **conservative** if:

- You'll need the money within 1–3 years
- You're financially supporting others right now

- You're in a high-uncertainty phase (visas, transfers, family health)
- You're easily stressed by losses

Your Portfolio Should Change As Your Season Changes

Early in your NIL journey? Build. Grow. Take some smart risks.

Mid-college? Balance growth with safety. Stay steady.

Graduating soon or about to go pro? Protect what you've earned.

Your financial strategy should evolve as your life evolves—just like your athletic role has changed over time.

Final Thoughts: Build a Legacy, Not Just a Moment

You didn't come this far just to flex on social media for one season. You came to make a difference—for yourself, your family, your country, and your future.

That means treating NIL money like the beginning, not the finish line.

Build a strong team. Diversify. Adjust your strategy based on your season. Don't panic during rough markets. Don't chase someone else's hot streak.

Stick to your playbook. Trust your training. Focus on long term wins.

Because when the dust settles and your career shifts—from college athlete to business leader, creator, or professional—you'll still have something solid.

You didn't just get paid.

You built something that lasts.

Chapter 35: The Eighth Wonder of the World – Understanding Compound Interest

Introduction: Why Time Is the Most Powerful Asset You Have

As an international student-athlete, you're already juggling school, sports, and life in a whole new country. Now you've got NIL income in the mix. And with it, the question: What should I do with this money?

Most people think building wealth requires a lot of money. The truth? It requires *time* and *consistency*. One of the most powerful forces in all of finance is something called **compound interest**—and if you start using it now, it could change the entire trajectory of your life.

Albert Einstein reportedly called compound interest the "eighth wonder of the world."

"He who understands it, earns it. He who doesn't, pays it."

Whether or not he actually said that doesn't matter—because the principle is 100% true.

Compound interest can grow your NIL money exponentially. Or, if you're not careful, it can grow your *debt* just as fast. This chapter will show you how to make compound interest your teammate—not your opponent.

What Is Compound Interest?

Compound interest means earning interest on your original money *and* the interest that money earns over time.

In simple terms:

You make money on your money. Then you make more money on *that* money. And it keeps going.

Unlike simple interest (which only pays you on your initial deposit), compound interest grows faster and faster, because every year your balance gets bigger—and the interest applies to the whole thing.

It's like a snowball rolling downhill. Small at first, but eventually massive.

Example:

You invest $1,000 at 10% annual interest.

- Year 1: You earn $100. Your balance is $1,100.
- Year 2: You earn $110. Balance: $1,210.
- Year 3: You earn $121. Balance: $1,331.
- By year 10? You're over $2,500.
- By year 20? You're over $6,700.
- And you never added another dollar.

That's the magic of compounding.

Why Compound Interest Matters for You—Right Now

As a young athlete, you have something most people don't: **time**. And with compound interest, time is the most powerful ingredient.

Even small investments now can grow into large amounts later—if you give them time.

Let's compare two athletes:

- Athlete A starts investing $200/month at age 18 and stops at age 28. That's 10 years, $24,000 total.

- Athlete B waits until age 28 and invests $200/month until age 65. That's 37 years, $88,800 total.

Who ends up with more money at age 65 (assuming an 8% return)?

Athlete A.

Why? Because their money had more time to grow.

Time Beats Timing

Some people try to "time the market"—waiting for the perfect moment to invest.

That's a mistake.

Time in the market is what matters. The longer your money is invested, the more it grows. The best time to start was yesterday. The second-best time? Today.

The Rule of 72 – Quick Math for Doubling Money

Want to know how long it takes for your money to double? Use the **Rule of 72**:

Divide 72 by your expected interest rate.

Examples:

- 72 ÷ 6% = 12 years to double
- 72 ÷ 9% = 8 years
- 72 ÷ 12% = 6 years

So if you invest $10,000 at 9%, in about 8 years you'll have $20,000.

In 16 years, $40,000.

In 24 years, $80,000.

And you didn't add another cent.

Why Waiting Hurts – The Compound Timeline

Let's say three international athletes invest $100/month at 8% return:

- Start at age 18: ~$351,428 by age 65
- Start at age 28: ~$164,870
- Start at age 38: ~$74,336

Waiting just 10 years could cost you nearly $200,000. That's why starting now matters.

Where to Use Compound Interest (Even on a Student Visa)

You don't need to be a U.S. citizen to benefit from compound interest. But you do need to be aware of which accounts you're eligible for.

Visa and tax status matter. You may need to file as a "non-resident alien" or use international-friendly platforms.

Here are your main options:

Roth IRA

- Grows tax-free
- Withdrawals are tax-free
- Must have earned income
- You may need to establish residency or meet specific visa rules

Caution: Many international students can't legally contribute to IRAs unless they meet certain tax residency rules. Check with a CPA who understands student visas.

Brokerage Accounts

- No contribution limits
- Invest in stocks, ETFs, mutual funds
- Pay taxes on gains
- More flexible and accessible

Best option for many international athletes. No need for U.S. citizenship—just proper paperwork and a valid ITIN (Individual Taxpayer Identification Number) or SSN.

High-Yield Savings

- Not exciting, but earns interest
- Safe and accessible
- No investment risk

Great for emergency funds or short-term savings—not for long-term wealth.

Compound Interest Can Work Against You Too

Here's the other side of the story: compound interest doesn't just apply to savings and investments. It also applies to **debt**—especially **credit cards** and high-interest loans.

That means you can go into debt faster than you think.

Example:

You borrow $5,000 at 22% interest on a credit card.

If you only make minimum payments, you could end up paying *double* that amount over time.

That's compound interest working *against* you.

Avoiding the Trap: Don't Let Debt Compound

To make compound interest your friend—not your enemy:

- Pay off credit cards in full every month
- Avoid payday loans or high-interest borrowing
- Only finance what you *absolutely* need
- Invest early and often—even small amounts
- Automate savings so you don't forget

Think Like an Investor, Not a Spender

When NIL money hits your account, it's tempting to spend. That's human. But every dollar you spend now is a dollar that *won't* grow later.

Ask yourself:

- Will this help me grow long-term?
- Am I giving this dollar a job—or letting it disappear?
- Can I invest it now and thank myself later?

Compound interest is like planting a tree. You don't get shade immediately—but one day, you'll be *so* glad you planted it.

Getting Started: Your First Steps

1. **Open a brokerage account** – Look for international-friendly platforms like Charles Schwab, Interactive Brokers, or international accounts with Fidelity.
2. **Start small** – Even $25–$100/month can make a difference.
3. **Pick a low-cost index fund** – Total Market or S&P 500 funds are great places to begin.
4. **Automate your contributions** – Make investing a habit.
5. **Leave it alone** – Let time and compound interest do the work.

6. **Increase your contribution when you earn more** – Pay yourself first.

Final Thoughts: Make Compound Interest Your Teammate

As an athlete, you understand long-term focus. You train today for success tomorrow. You show up every day even when results don't come right away.

That's compound interest.

It rewards discipline. It rewards patience. And it rewards the athlete who thinks long-term—not just season to season, but year to year.

NIL is your moment to shine. But wealth? Wealth is what happens when you let part of that shine *compound* in the background.

You don't need to be rich to start.

You just need to start.

Chapter 36: The Power of No – Protecting Your Peace and Your Pockets

Introduction: When the Checks Start Coming In, So Do the Requests

When the NIL money starts flowing, it's exciting. You're signing endorsement deals, making money through content, merchandise, appearances, and sponsorships. But just as real as the income is the pressure. The calls and texts start coming in. Family members you love ask for "just a little help." Friends expect you to cover dinner, buy gear, or invest in their "big idea." Old contacts come out of nowhere with financial needs or business pitches.

Saying "no" in these moments isn't being cold—it's being smart. It's not just about protecting money, it's about protecting your future, your mental health, and your peace of mind. This chapter will help you learn how to say no clearly, kindly, and confidently—without guilt.

Why It's Hard to Say "No"

Let's start with the truth: for many student-athletes, especially first-generation wealth earners, success isn't seen as just personal—it's a win for the entire family. It can feel like everyone is depending on you. Maybe you:

- Feel like the "chosen one" expected to lift everyone up
- Want to give back out of gratitude
- Feel guilty for having something others don't
- Think people won't understand if you say no

These emotions are valid. But always saying yes—especially when you can't afford to—doesn't help anyone in the long run. You didn't work hard just to become someone else's safety net. You worked hard to build a life of freedom and opportunity. Protect that.

The Real Cost of Always Saying Yes

Handing out money feels good in the short term. You feel generous. You feel needed. You feel like you're doing right by people who matter to you. But here's what often happens over time:

- Your finances start slipping—savings disappear, bills pile up, and you fall behind on your own goals.
- People get used to the handouts. What felt like help becomes an expectation.
- You find it hard to say no later. And when you finally do, people react negatively.
- Resentment grows. You feel used, and they feel entitled.

Always saying yes creates a pattern. You stop investing in yourself. You become the plan for everyone else. But who is helping you?

What to Say Instead of "No"

Saying "no" doesn't have to be rude or aggressive. You can communicate boundaries with kindness, clarity, and firmness. Here are some ways to say no—without feeling like a bad person:

- "I've already committed my money to a financial plan. Everything's accounted for."
- "I'm trying to build something that lasts. I can't give out money right now."
- "I've talked with my advisor, and right now I'm not in a position to help."
- "I love you, but I'm not loaning or gifting money to anyone right now."
- "I can't give you money, but I'm happy to support you in other ways."

Here's a tip: blame the plan, not the person. Instead of making it about their request being unreasonable, make it about your plan being the priority. You aren't rejecting them—you're sticking to your structure.

Enabling vs. Empowering

Let's say you help someone out. Maybe you pay a car note or cover rent one month. It feels good. But what happens next month? And the month after that?

If you give money without teaching financial skills, you're not helping—you're enabling. That means you're creating a dependency. Now, instead of solving a problem, you've just delayed it and trained someone to come to you again.

Empowering someone is different. It looks like:

- Helping them get a job or build a budget
- Encouraging them to learn about money
- Offering guidance instead of a handout
- Supporting their growth, not just their survival

Handouts end. Education multiplies.

You Are Not Their Financial Plan

If someone's entire financial recovery depends on *you*, that's a problem. You are not their emergency fund, retirement plan, or financial institution.

Here are some boundaries that protect you:

- No loans, no exceptions
- No gifts unless it's budgeted and doesn't hurt you
- No investing in someone else's business without full due diligence
- No cosigning or opening credit in your name for anyone

If you decide to help, do it intentionally and once—not habitually and out of guilt.

Legacy Over Likes

A lot of athletes fall into the trap of being liked. They want to be seen as generous, successful, and loyal. But being liked by everyone can leave you broke. What matters more than likes is legacy.

Legacy is what you leave behind—wealth, wisdom, and example. Protecting your money now means being able to:

- Buy your first home
- Invest in a business of your own
- Support your future kids
- Take care of your parents in retirement
- Give back to your community in bigger ways later

Saying no today might hurt someone's feelings. But saying yes and ending up broke helps no one.

When You're the First to Make It

Being the first in your family or community to have money is a beautiful but heavy role. You feel the pressure to give back. You feel the eyes on you. You feel like if you don't help, no one will.

But remember:

- You help people best when you're stable yourself.
- You can't give from an empty account.
- Just because you're first doesn't mean you're responsible for everyone else's success.

You can inspire others by showing what responsible money looks like. That example is worth more than any handout.

Boundaries Are Not Betrayal

Let's get something straight: saying no is not betrayal. It's self-respect. Setting boundaries doesn't make you cold, distant, or selfish. It means you know where your limits are.

Saying no now may mean fewer calls, fewer messages, or some awkward silence. That's okay. People who love you will understand. And if they don't, that tells you something too.

Boundaries protect your ability to keep showing up—for yourself, and one day, for others who *truly* need it.

Create a Script

Don't wait until you're put on the spot. Have a go-to response ready for when people ask for money.

Here's a script:

"I've created a financial plan for my income, and I'm not giving out any money right now. I hope you understand. I'm focused on building something long-term."

Or:

"I've made the decision not to lend or give money to friends or family. It's a personal boundary I'm holding to make sure I stay on track."

You can adjust the tone based on who you're talking to—but keep the boundary firm.

Help Without Giving Money

Sometimes you want to help—but not with cash. That's a great instinct. Here's how you can still be supportive:

- Recommend a job lead or resource
- Help someone budget or apply for assistance
- Introduce them to a mentor or advisor
- Give them books or podcasts on financial literacy
- Offer your time or emotional support instead

Money isn't the only way to care.

If You Do Say Yes, Do It Right

If you decide to help someone financially, set clear terms:

- Be specific about the amount
- Make it a one-time gift, not a recurring expectation
- If it's a loan, write it down and agree on a repayment timeline
- Say, "This is a one-time thing," and stick to it

Helping someone once doesn't mean you're now responsible for them. Be generous on your terms—not theirs.

Know the Red Flags

Some people won't take no for an answer. Watch for:

- Guilt-tripping: "But you owe me after everything I did for you."
- Pressure: "You have the money, why not help?"
- Repeated asks: "Just this one more time…"
- Manipulation: "If you really loved me, you'd do this."

These are signs someone may be more interested in your money than your well-being. Don't fall for it.

What Happens If You Don't Learn to Say No

Many athletes give and give—until there's nothing left.

They sign great deals, but they never build anything for themselves.

They support everyone except the one person who earned it: themselves.

Then the deals dry up. The attention fades. And the money's gone.

And suddenly, all the people who were always around… disappear.

Learn to say no now, so that when the spotlight dims, you're still standing on something solid.

Closing Thoughts: Say No Now, So You Can Say Yes Later

Saying no today protects your ability to say yes tomorrow.

Yes to a house.

Yes to investing.

Yes to giving generously—when you're in a place to do it.

Yes to building real wealth.

Yes to your own dreams.

Don't let short-term pressure ruin your long-term vision. You are not just someone's ATM. You are a brand, a business, and a future success story in the making.

Protect your peace. Guard your generosity. Lead with wisdom.
And always remember: *"No" is a complete sentence.*

Chapter 30: You Made It Here—Now Make It Count: The Legacy of NIL Starts With You

If you've made it to this point in the book, take a moment and let that sink in.

You've done something most student-athletes—**especially international student-athletes**—never get the chance to do: you've taken time to understand the system behind the spotlight. You've peeled back the curtain on what Name, Image, and Likeness really means—not just for your wallet, but for your future. You've tackled visas and taxes, banking and branding, culture and contracts, influence and investment.

Now what?

This final chapter isn't about new concepts or complicated strategies. It's about what comes next. It's about **owning everything you've learned**, using it, sharing it, and carrying it with you into every season—on and off the field, in and out of the classroom, across every border.

Whether NIL turns into your side hustle, your business, or your springboard into something greater, this chapter is your reminder: **you are the opportunity.** Your journey, your perspective, your name—it's all currency.

But currency only matters if you use it wisely.

Let's talk about how.

SECTION ONE: WHY THIS MOMENT MATTERS MORE THAN YOU THINK

It's easy to treat NIL like a temporary bonus—a side project while you're focused on school or sport. And yes, for some, that's all it will be.

But for others—maybe *you*—it's the beginning of something generational.

This is more than a chance to make some extra money while you compete. This is a moment in history when the rules changed, and for the first time, athletes from around the world could finally say, *"My name matters. My image matters. My story matters."*

For international students, this moment is even more rare.

You didn't grow up in this system. You didn't get the same workshops, guidance counselors, or NIL-ready families many U.S. students did. You probably had to figure out things solo—applying for your visa, navigating a new culture, adjusting to new expectations.

And yet, here you are.

You've stepped into the American college sports system—a place of possibility, pressure, politics, and performance—and now you're stepping into **the business of you.**

Whether you become a professional athlete, a business leader, or an advocate for the next generation, your NIL experience can be the **training ground for long-term success.**

SECTION TWO: WHAT YOU KNOW NOW

Let's zoom out and reflect on everything you've learned in this book.

You now understand:

- The rules that apply to your visa and what NIL activity is legally allowed
- How to open and manage a U.S. bank account
- The basics of taxes, investment accounts, and the power of starting early
- The risks and red flags in contracts, agents, and shady partnerships

- How your personal brand can either open doors or limit you
- How to protect your mental health in a high-pressure, public-facing environment
- What to watch for in your home country (cross-border taxation, currency exchange, and expectations to give back)
- How to be smart about spending, peer pressure, and lifestyle inflation
- How to connect your values to your vision
- How to build relationships, network with integrity, and leave a lasting impact

That's not just NIL literacy—that's **life literacy**.

This isn't about making one good deal. This is about learning how to make **decisions that hold up under pressure.** You've got the tools now.

SECTION THREE: YOU ARE THE BRAND, BUT YOU ARE NOT FOR SALE

Let's be clear—**you are not just your NIL.** You're not just a body on a poster, a handle on a platform, or a stat on a roster.

You are a person.

And when NIL starts to feel like pressure, like performance, like you always have to smile, post, promote, and perform—**pause.** Come back to your core.

Your worth is not in your followers, your engagement, your sponsorships, or even your sport. It's in your identity, your values, and the people you impact along the way.

The best NIL brands are the ones that feel **real.** Not the flashiest. Not the loudest. Not the ones with the biggest chains or the wildest giveaways. The ones that speak with purpose. The ones that make people stop scrolling and start thinking. The ones that reflect the athlete behind the name.

You're allowed to build a brand *and* set boundaries. You can say yes to the bag *and* say no to anything that doesn't align with your story.

Remember: **you're not just in the NIL business. You're in the integrity business.**

SECTION FOUR: MONEY IS A TOOL, NOT A TEST

Let's talk about the money.

Yes, NIL can bring income. For some, it may be a few hundred dollars. For others, tens of thousands. But either way, **money doesn't change who you are—it reveals who you are.**

If you make $500 and blow it on clout, you'd blow $5,000 the same way. If you save $50 now, you'll be ready to invest $5,000 later.

The money you earn through NIL isn't just payment—it's practice. This is your shot to learn how to budget, how to save, how to invest, how to say no, how to research, and how to **stay in control of your future—even when everyone wants a piece of you.**

And here's the key: **you don't have to be rich to be ready.**

Read that again.

The habits you build today—tracking your spending, thinking long-term, asking questions—those habits will serve you whether you're an All-American or an everyday pro. Whether you return home or stay stateside. Whether you go big or go quiet.

Money doesn't make you smarter. But learning how to manage money? **That will always put you ahead.**

SECTION FIVE: GIVE BACK WITHOUT GIVING YOURSELF AWAY

Many international athletes feel pressure to "make it" for their family, their village, their hometown, their country. And there's nothing wrong with that. That's beautiful.

But don't forget: **you matter, too.**

You can't pour into your community if your own cup is empty. You can't lead others if you haven't learned how to lead yourself. Giving back isn't just about sending money home. It's about bringing *wisdom* back. Bringing tools. Resources. Options. A new mindset.

This book is part of your legacy. You now carry information that your younger siblings, teammates, and community members might never get. So share it. Talk about it. Teach it. Be the bridge.

But don't let guilt, pressure, or pride drive you into decisions that hurt you financially or emotionally. You are not obligated to sacrifice your peace for other people's expectations.

Give from overflow, not from survival.

SECTION SIX: LIFE AFTER COLLEGE—THE REAL ENDGAME

No matter how your athletic career ends—on a championship podium, after an injury, or quietly after graduation—life will keep going.

NIL is temporary. Your education, your values, your financial literacy, and your relationships—**those last.**

Start thinking now about what's next:

- Will you stay in the U.S. or return home?
- Will you apply for Optional Practical Training (OPT) or explore professional leagues abroad?
- Will you start a business, go to grad school, or work in your field of study?
- How will your brand continue beyond your sport?

This book wasn't written to help you be famous in college. It was written to help you build a life of purpose and options long after the cheering stops.

SECTION SEVEN: A FINAL WORD TO THE WORLD CHANGER

So here we are.

You're no longer just a student-athlete. You're not just an international athlete. You're someone with a financial playbook, a personal brand, a sense of ownership over your decisions, and a vision that can stretch across oceans and borders.

You are living proof that NIL is about more than just sports. It's about **equity, access, education, and power.**

You now understand contracts, cash flow, taxes, visas, social media, mental health, and investing—at an age where most people don't know the difference between a debit card and a credit score.

That's rare.

And rare becomes powerful when it's intentional.

So be intentional. With your name. With your image. With your decisions. With your circle. With your legacy.

This book may be over—but your story is just beginning.

Don't just be part of the NIL era. Define it.

Stay hungry. Stay humble. Stay wise.

And wherever you go from here—go boldly.

— *Pat Brown, MBA*

Disclaimer

The information provided in this book is for educational purposes only and is not intended as legal, financial, tax, immigration, or investment advice. While every effort has been made to ensure the accuracy of the content at the time of publication, laws, regulations, and individual circumstances may change. Readers are encouraged to consult with qualified professionals—including financial advisors, tax professionals, immigration attorneys, and compliance officers—before making decisions related to Name, Image, and Likeness (NIL) activities.

This book does not create a client relationship between the author and reader, nor does it guarantee specific outcomes. Every student-athlete's situation is unique, especially international students who may be subject to specific visa and immigration restrictions. Always check with your university's compliance office and legal counsel to ensure that your NIL activities are compliant with school policies and federal immigration regulations.

While real-life examples, templates, and suggestions are included for context, they should not be interpreted as personalized advice or endorsements of any specific product, service, or platform.

If you have questions or would like to explore working directly with the author, you may contact Patrick Brown, MBA, at [insert your preferred contact information or website].

Questions to ask

10 Questions to Ask a Financial Advisor (as an International Student-Athlete)

1. **How can I manage my NIL income while staying compliant with my F-1 visa restrictions?**
2. **What's the best way to budget my monthly expenses with fluctuating NIL income?**
3. **Should I save money in a U.S. account, my home country, or both?**
4. **Can I start investing while I'm in the U.S. as an international student?**
5. **How do I build credit responsibly in the U.S. without taking on unnecessary debt?**
6. **What type of financial tools (checking, savings, apps, etc.) do you recommend for tracking my money?**
7. **How should I allocate my NIL earnings—how much should I save, spend, and give?**
8. **What financial risks should I be aware of as an international athlete earning NIL income?**
9. **Can you help me plan for my future if I stay in the U.S. or return home after graduation?**
10. **How do I set financial goals that align with my short-term college experience and long-term career aspirations?**

10 Questions to Ask a CPA (Certified Public Accountant)

1. **Do I need to file a U.S. tax return even if I only earned a small amount of NIL income?**
2. **What tax forms should I use as a non-resident international student (e.g., 1040-NR)?**
3. **Will I owe taxes on NIL income earned through social media or product endorsements?**
4. **Am I subject to tax withholding, and how do I know how much to set aside for taxes?**
5. **Can you help me avoid double taxation with my home country?**
6. **Do I qualify for any tax deductions or exemptions as an international student?**
7. **How should I document and report NIL-related expenses (travel, gear, marketing, etc.)?**
8. **Can you help me get an Individual Taxpayer Identification Number (ITIN) if I don't have a Social Security Number?**
9. **What happens if I don't file taxes correctly or miss a deadline?**
10. **How can I prepare for a tax audit or investigation if I'm selected for one?**

10 Questions to Ask an Attorney (Immigration, Contract, or Business)

For an Immigration Attorney:

1. **What NIL activities are allowed under an F-1 visa—and which could put me at risk?**
2. **Can I legally promote brands or products on social media while on a student visa?**
3. **What should I know about CPT, OPT, and other post-graduation options if I want to stay in the U.S.?**
4. **How do I avoid accidentally violating the "employment" rules tied**

to my visa?

5. **What are the consequences if I break NIL-related immigration laws?**

For a Contract/Business Attorney:

1. **What red flags should I look for in NIL contracts, sponsorships, or brand agreements?**
2. **Should I form a business (like an LLC) for my NIL income, and is that legal under my visa?**
3. **Can I sign a deal with an agent or rep, and what should I expect in that contract?**
4. **How can I protect my image, name, and brand legally in both the U.S. and my home country?**
5. **Can you help me review NIL deals before I sign them—even if they seem small?**

Important Financial Dates for International Students

1. January 1 – New Financial Year Begins

- Start organizing documents from the previous year.
- Begin tracking NIL income, expenses, and receipts for taxes.
- Update your financial goals or budget for the new year.

2. January 31 – Deadline for Form 1042-S / W-2 / 1099

- If you earned income (through NIL, school jobs, or U.S.-based companies), you may receive:
- **Form 1042-S** (common for international students)
- **Form W-2** (for school-related jobs)
- **Form 1099** (if you worked as an independent contractor)
- These are used to prepare your U.S. tax return.

3. February – Apply for ITIN (If You Don't Have an SSN)

- If you're earning money but not eligible for a Social Security Number, apply for an **Individual Taxpayer Identification Number (ITIN)** using **Form W-7**.
- Required for filing taxes or opening some financial accounts.

4. March 15 – U.S. Business Tax Return Deadline (for LLCs or Partnerships)

- If you created a U.S. business entity (e.g., an LLC for NIL income), you may need to file **Form 1065** or **1120S** by this date.

5. April 15 – Federal Tax Return Deadline (Form 1040-NR or 8843)

- Most international students must file:
- **Form 1040-NR** (Non-Resident Income Tax Return), **and**
- **Form 8843** (even if you earned no U.S. income)
- Check for deadline changes; it sometimes extends to **April 18**.

6. June 15 – Tax Filing Deadline for Non-Residents Abroad

- If you're back in your home country or have foreign residence, you may qualify for an automatic 2-month extension.

7. July–August – Plan Financial Aid or Campus Job Renewal

- Renew on-campus employment (if allowed).
- Plan housing and tuition expenses for the next academic year.
- Revisit your U.S. budget and currency exchange strategies.

8. September – Begin Financial Planning for Next Year

- Begin tracking income/expenses again for the next tax cycle.
- Evaluate summer income, NIL deals, or travel costs.
- Consider back-to-school budgeting and savings goals.

9. October 1 – FAFSA Opens (for U.S. Citizens/Green Card Holders)

- Not typically applicable to international students, but helpful if you plan to become a permanent resident or have mixed-status family members.

10. December 31 – Finalize Year-End Financial Activities

- Last day to make tax-deductible donations or business purchases (if applicable).
- Finalize recordkeeping for NIL income or student job earnings.
- Reflect on your financial wins and set goals for the new year.

Bonus: Visa-Specific Dates

While not money-focused, these impact your financial life:

- **End of OPT/CPT Period** – Triggers end of legal work eligibility
- **Grace Period Expiration (Usually 60 Days)** – After F-1 program ends
- **SEVIS Fee Deadlines** – Before visa renewals or changes

Money & Banking Terms

1. **Budget** – A plan for how to spend, save, and manage your money based on income and expenses.
2. **Savings Account** – A bank account where money earns interest over time and is used for saving, not spending.
3. **Checking Account** – A bank account used for everyday expenses like rent, groceries, and bills.
4. **Emergency Fund** – Money set aside for unexpected expenses (medical bills, travel, job loss).
5. **Currency Exchange Rate** – The value of one country's currency in relation to another.
6. **Remittance** – Money sent by a person working abroad (like a student) to family in their home country.
7. **Overdraft Fee** – A penalty charged when you spend more than what's in your bank account.
8. **Wire Transfer** – A method of electronically transferring money, often used internationally.

Financial Growth & Credit

1. **Credit Score** – A number (300–850) that shows how reliable you are at repaying money (not common for new international students).
2. **Credit Report** – A record of your credit activity and payment history.
3. **Interest** – The cost of borrowing money (or the money you earn from saving/investing).
4. **Compound Interest** – Interest earned on both the original amount

and the interest it accumulates.

5. **APR (Annual Percentage Rate)** – The yearly cost of borrowing money, expressed as a percentage.
6. **Debt** – Money you owe and must repay.
7. **Loan** – Money borrowed that must be repaid, usually with interest.
8. **Net Worth** – Your total assets (what you own) minus liabilities (what you owe).

💼 NIL & Business Terms

1. **NIL (Name, Image, and Likeness)** – The right of an athlete to earn money from their personal brand.
2. **Endorsement** – A public approval or promotion of a product or service for compensation.
3. **Sponsorship** – A deal where a company supports an athlete financially or with products in exchange for promotion.
4. **Royalty** – A payment based on the sales of something using your name, image, or content.
5. **Independent Contractor** – A self-employed individual who earns income without being an employee.
6. **LLC (Limited Liability Company)** – A business structure that separates your personal and business assets.
7. **Agent** – A representative who negotiates deals or endorsements on your behalf.
8. **Contract** – A legal agreement between two or more parties that outlines rights and obligations.

Tax & Compliance Terms

1. **IRS (Internal Revenue Service)** – The U.S. government agency responsible for collecting taxes.
2. **Form 1040-NR** – The U.S. tax return form for non-resident international students.

3. **Form 8843** – A required form for international students to declare visa and presence in the U.S.
4. **ITIN (Individual Taxpayer Identification Number)** – A number used by non-residents to file taxes if they don't qualify for a Social Security Number.
5. **W-2 Form** – A form showing wages earned and taxes withheld (from on-campus jobs).
6. **1099 Form** – A tax form used for independent contractor income, common in NIL deals.
7. **Tax Treaty** – An agreement between two countries to prevent double taxation.
8. **Tax Deduction** – A reduction in taxable income that can lower your tax bill.

Immigration & Visa Terms

1. **F-1 Visa** – A nonimmigrant visa for full-time international students studying in the U.S.
2. **SEVIS** – The Student and Exchange Visitor Information System that tracks international students.
3. **CPT (Curricular Practical Training)** – Work authorization for international students tied to academic programs.
4. **OPT (Optional Practical Training)** – Work authorization after graduation (usually for 12 months).
5. **DSO (Designated School Official)** – A university official who helps international students maintain legal status.
6. **Grace Period** – The time allowed to remain in the U.S. after your program or OPT ends.
7. **Status Violation** – Breaking visa rules (like working without permission), which can lead to removal or visa issues.
8. **USCIS (U.S. Citizenship and Immigration Services)** – The agency that handles visa, immigration, and work authorization services.

About the Author

Patrick Brown, MBA, is a former Division I football captain, financial educator, and wealth manager with over two decades of experience helping individuals and families make smart, empowered financial decisions. After navigating his own journey from college athlete to professional football player to financial expert, Patrick saw a massive gap in financial education—especially for student-athletes, and even more so for international athletes facing the complexities of U.S. systems.

With firsthand knowledge of what it feels like to have visibility but little financial literacy, Patrick made it his mission to simplify money, taxes, branding, and business education for the next generation of athletes. He founded *Financial Literacy For NIL* and several other financial platforms to educate student-athletes on how to manage money wisely, understand the new landscape of NIL (Name, Image, and Likeness), and build sustainable wealth—no matter where their careers take them.

Patrick has spoken at universities, athletic programs, and community events across the country, and serves as a mentor to athletes, coaches, and parents alike. His financial literacy work bridges cultural, economic, and generational gaps, empowering young people with the tools and mindset to own their financial story.

As a former international-level competitor himself, Patrick deeply understands the unique challenges faced by international student-athletes: visa restrictions, tax complexities, cultural transitions, and the pressure of living far from home. This book is his way of giving back—and of helping athletes avoid the mistakes and confusion he once faced.

When he's not coaching clients or writing, Patrick enjoys time with his wife Cassandra and their two daughters, Peyton and Ryan. Whether on the field or in finance, Patrick believes in discipline, strategy, and most importantly—**knowing the playbook before you enter the game.**

Made in the USA
Monee, IL
04 November 2026

67387581R00138